Hacking the Case Interview:

Your Shortcut Guide to Mastering Consulting Interviews

Taylor Warfield

All rights reserved. No parts of this book may be reproduced or transmitted in any form by any means, including electronic, mechanical, photocopy, recording, or otherwise, without the prior written permission of the author.

Copyright © 2020 by Taylor Warfield

ISBN-13: 978-1545261828

ISBN-10: 1545261822

Table of Contents

Introduction 1
I. The Different Parts and Progression of a Case Interview 5
II. Understanding the Case Background Information 15
III. Verifying Objectives 21
IV. Developing a Structured Framework 25
V. Handling the Moment of Silence 37
VI. Presenting Your Framework 39
VII. Starting the Case 43
VIII. Solving Quantitative Problems 47
IX. Answering Qualitative Business Questions 61
X. Delivering a Conclusion 75
XI. Everything You Need to Memorize 79
Introduction to Doing Practice Cases 83
Practice Case #1 – It's Wine O'Clock Somewhere 85
Practice Case #2 – Clothes Woes 97
Practice Case #3 – Let's Bank on It 111
Practice Case #4 – The Price is Right 125
Practice Case #5 – Diamonds are Forever 139
Final Thoughts 153
About the Author 155

Introduction

What is a case interview?

If you are reading this book, you are likely preparing for an upcoming consulting case interview. Whether your case interview is months away or even tomorrow, this book is designed to teach you how to confidently and effectively master case interviews in a clear, concise, and direct way.

Why do consulting companies give case interviews to their candidates? The primary reason is that case interviews are the most effective way to help companies determine if a candidate will be successful at the consulting job. During a case interview, candidates will be asked to solve broad business problems that real consultants solve in the real world. For example, should a laptop manufacturer enter the tablet market? How should a hotel price its different rooms? Should a large, declining pharmaceutical company acquire a smaller, more innovative healthcare startup? These broad business problems that real consultants spend months solving, you will solve in a 30 minute to one-hour case interview.

Case interviews test for problem solving skills, the ability to communicate clearly and effectively, business acumen, and enthusiasm for consulting all at once. There are so many different capabilities and qualities that interviewers are looking for. Case interviews also give you a taste of what it is like to be a consultant. If you enjoy doing case interviews, there is a high chance that you will also enjoy the consulting job.

A typical McKinsey, Bain, or BCG first-round interview is comprised of two back-to-back case interviews while a final-round may have two to four case interviews. To get a job offer from a top consulting firm, you will need to nail four to six case interviews each time.

The purpose of this book

When I was interviewing for consulting, I read nearly every single case interview book on the market. For these books, I felt that only 20% of the content had valuable information while the other 80% was filled with common sense suggestions, anecdotal stories, or long rambling narratives. Even though these books had 250+ pages, I felt they were missing a lot of the precise details that separate a good case interview candidate from an exceptional one. I would spend a week reading a case interview book, only to finish with knowledge that I could have learned in a single day, while also missing the details needed to be exceptional.

I wanted this book to be different.

My aspiration for writing this book is to give you everything you need to know to master case interviews in the shortest amount of time possible. To do this, I cut out all of the useless fluff and narratives that other books sell you and try to keep my prose as direct, clear, and concise as possible. I will tell you exactly what you need to do and say, what the interviewer is looking for, and how to differentiate yourself from the thousands of other candidates every single step of the way.

With that said, reading this book by itself will not make you a case interview master. To achieve full mastery, you will need to spend many more hours practicing mock case interviews. There is no book that can teach you everything that you learn from doing practice case interviews. Practice and discipline will get you multiple consulting job offers.

This book will answer a variety of different questions that you may have:

- What should I expect during a case interview?

- What should I do and say during each part of the case interview?

- What is the interviewer looking for in each part of the case interview?

- What business knowledge do I need to know?

- What kinds of math should I be able to do?

- What frameworks do I need to memorize?

- How do I differentiate myself from the thousands of other candidates?

- How do I do practice case interviews to get better?

If you find this book helpful and want even more detailed explanations, examples, practice problems, real practice cases, and strategies to differentiate yourself, I've created a one-week online crash course that can be found at **HackingTheCaseInterview.com**. I'll provide more details on this in part XI: "Everything You Need to Memorize."

Who am I?

By the time I had finished interviewing with consulting firms, I had done and given 200+ practice cases and had interviewed at over ten different firms. My hard work paid off, as I received multiple offers and ended up signing with Bain & Company. In my first few years of work, I led case interview workshops across schools in the US and gave many case interviews. I worked with high-potential candidates, and helped many of them receive job offers.

This book is a compilation of all of the hundreds of hours of case interview experience I have accumulated. I hope that this book will help you receive your dream job offer.

Let's get started.

I. The Different Parts and Progression of a Case Interview

With enough practice, case interviews can be straight forward and even repetitive. Every single case roughly follows this one particular sequence. It's all about knowing what to expect during each part of the case interview and being prepared for each part.

The rest of the book is organized into chapters by these different parts of a case interview. Each chapter will discuss the following: what happens during each part of the case interview, what the interviewer is looking for, exactly what you should be doing, and how to differentiate yourself from the thousands of other candidates out there that are interviewing for the same position.

How the case interview will proceed

Interviewer: Presents background information on the case, what the problem is, and what the objective or objectives are
(II. Understanding the Case Background Information)

You: Synthesize major points of the case background information and verify objectives
(III. Verifying Objectives)

You: Request time to structure thoughts into a framework
(IV. Developing a Structured Framework)

***Silence for two to three minutes
(V. Handling the Moment of Silence)

You: Present framework to interviewer
(VI. Presenting your Framework)

You + Interviewer: Either the interviewer will review your framework and suggest an area to start the case OR you will be expected to suggest an area to start the case
(VII. Starting the Case)

You + Interviewer: Solving quantitative problems
(VIII. Solving Quantitative Problems)

You + Interviewer: Solving qualitative questions on business judgement/intuition
(IX. Answering Qualitative Business Questions)

You + Interviewer: The interviewer will ask or prompt you for a summary and recommendation
(X. Delivering a Conclusion)

What else to expect during a case interview

For the majority of the case interview, both you and the interviewer will be working together to reach the ultimate answer. Think of the case interview as a flowing discussion of ideas and opinions. The case interview should not sound like a Q&A session. Even for the sections above that are not marked "You + Interviewer," you should still be engaged with the interviewer, asking questions, aligning on the path forward, and asking for input.

There will be times during the case interview when the interviewer will be driving the case and guiding you on what direction the case interview should proceed. They will be asking you questions to answer and giving you information along the way. Other times, you will be driving and leading the case interview. You will be expected to ask the interviewer for information and suggest areas to look into or analyze.

During the case interview, don't be surprised if the interviewer gives you handouts with charts, graphs, tables, or other forms of data. They are testing for your ability to interpret and analyze data, a critical capability for any consultant.

Finally, do not bring a calculator, reference books, or notes to the case interview. All math that you do will be calculated by hand, and the interviewer will not let you refer to external materials. The only notes that you should have are the ones that you are taking during the case interview.

To give you a better idea of what a case interview sounds like, I am including a full case interview dialogue below. While reading the dialogue, pay close attention to how collaborative and discussion-based the interview is.

Example of a full case interview dialogue

Interviewer: Our client is Burger Guys, a fast food burger restaurant that sells hamburgers, cheeseburgers, and french fries. The CEO of the restaurant has hired us because they have been losing money over the past year. He wants to know why Burger Guys is losing money, and what they should do about it.

Candidate: Great. To clarify, when you say that "Burger Guys is losing money," do you mean that profits have gone down? Or do you mean profitability has gone down?

Interviewer: Profits have gone down. Thanks for catching that.

Candidate: One other follow-up question, is Burger Guys a single restaurant? Or is it a chain with multiple locations?

Interviewer: Burger Guys is a single restaurant.

Candidate: Thanks. To summarize, our client is Burger Guys, a fast food burger restaurant that has experienced declining profits over the past year. The objectives of this case are to: 1) determine why Burger Guys is losing money, and 2) determine what Burger Guys should do to improve profits. Is my understanding correct?

Interviewer: Yes, it is.

Candidate: Would you mind if I took a moment to structure my thoughts and develop a framework that we can talk through to tackle the objectives?

Interviewer: Sure. That sounds great.

Candidate: Thanks.

***Silence for two to three minutes

Candidate: I am just about wrapping up my thoughts.

Interviewer: Take your time.

Candidate: In order to approach this problem, I would like to look into four areas.

First, I'd like to look at profit, and break it down into revenue and costs. I would like to look into how revenue and costs have changed over the past few years. Depending on which is most responsible for the decline in profits, I would like to further break down revenue (into quantity and price) and costs (into fixed costs and variable costs) to identify the specific drivers causing the decline in profits.

Second, I'd like to look into the different customer segments. Have customer preferences changed during this time period? Do customers perceive or view our company differently than before?

Third, I'd like to look into the competitive landscape of the fast food burger market. Have new competitors entered the market? Are competitors doing something different than what they were previously doing?

Fourth, I'd like to look into the fast food burger market itself. Have profits gone down for the fast food burger market overall? Are there new government regulations affecting burger production or selling? Are there new technologies or practices that are disrupting the fast food burger market?

Interviewer: That sounds good. I think all of the points you mentioned are relevant and worth looking into. Where would you like to start?

Candidate: I'd like to start with the first area, profit. I want to identify exactly why profits have gone done. After that, we can look into qualitatively why this is happening, and think through strategies and actions to address the decline in profits.

Interviewer: That makes sense. Let's proceed.

Candidate: Let's start with costs. Perhaps costs have gone up, which would cut into profits. Do we have any information on costs?

Interviewer: We don't have much information on costs. We believe that costs have not changed much in the past few years.

Candidate: Ok, since costs have roughly stayed the same, and profits have declined, that means revenue must have decreased. Do we have information on how quantity of food sold has changed? Or if we have changed price?

Interviewer: We have not changed price, but we have seen a decline in quantity sold.

Candidate: I know that we sell three different food items: hamburgers, cheeseburgers, and french fries. Is there a particular food item that has declined significantly in quantity sold?

Interviewer: We are seeing the steepest decline in hamburgers and cheeseburgers.

Candidate: Interesting. We have identified the driver behind the decline in profits. We are selling fewer hamburgers and cheeseburgers. The next step here is to look into why, qualitatively, are we selling fewer quantities of these food items? I think it would make sense to move onto the second area of my framework, customer segments. Do we have any information on what the different customer segments are, have their preferences changed over time, or if they view our company differently than before?

Interviewer: We do a customer food preference survey every year to understand customer demands and trends on various food items. Our survey produced the following information. What insights are you able to draw from this?

Question: What food are you most interested in eating?		
Food Item	Last Year: # of Respondents	This Year: # of Respondents
Burgers	12	18
Pizzas	7	14
Sandwiches	4	6
Other	2	2
Total	25	40

Candidate: Looking at this chart, I need to calculate the percentage of respondents that are most interested in eating each type of food since the survey totals for the two years aren't the same. Doing this, we see that customer preferences for burgers has gone down from 48% to 45%. Preferences for pizza have gone up from 28% to 35%. Preferences for sandwiches have gone down from 16% to 15% and the "Other" category has gone down from 8% to 5%. Therefore, I think that the decrease in sales of burgers is caused by a shift in customer preference towards eating pizza.

Interviewer: I agree with that interpretation. Let's say that management is interested in opening up a fast food pizza restaurant to take advantage of this change in customer preference. The first step in evaluating this is to determine the market size of pizzas. How would you go about calculating this?

Candidate: Before I start, I am assuming that we are defining the market as people in the US? Or is our fast food restaurant located in a different country?

Interviewer: Yes, let's go with the US.

Candidate: Would you mind if I took a minute to develop a structure for calculating this?

Interviewer: Of course, go ahead.

***Roughly a minute of silence

Candidate: In order to calculate the market size of pizzas in the US, I will first start with the US population. I will then segment the population by age group because different age groups have different levels of preference for eating pizza. Next, I will estimate the percentage of people in each age group that eat pizza. Once I have done this, I will estimate the frequency in which people eat pizza. This will give me the number of pizzas consumed in a year, and I will then multiply number of pizzas consumed with price to get the market size. How does that sound?

Interviewer: That sounds like a good approach. Let's proceed.

Candidate: Great. I will start off with the US population being 320M. I will then divide the population into four different age groups: (0-20), (20-40), (40-60), (60-80). This means each age group has 80M people.

Interviewer: What underlying assumptions are you making here?

Candidate: This assumes human life expectancy is 80 years, and I have assumed there is an even distribution of ages across the population. Does that seem reasonable?

Interviewer: Yes, that seems reasonable. I just wanted to make sure I caught all of your implicit assumptions.

Candidate: Looking at the (0-20) age group, I will assume a fairly high percentage eat pizza, since pizza seems to be very popular with kids and young adults. Let's assume 50% will eat pizza. This gives us 40M pizza consumers in this segment.

For the (20-40) age group, I think the percentage that eat pizza will be lower since this age group will be more concerned with their health and eating right. Let's assume 30% will eat pizza. This gives us 24M pizza consumers in this segment.

For the (40-60) age group, I would imagine that the percentage of people that eat pizza here is even lower. As people get older, I don't think their bodies will be able to process and digest pizza as easily as they could when they were younger. Let's assume 20% eat pizza. This gives us 16M pizza consumers in this segment.

Finally, for the (60-80) age group, I would imagine very few people eat pizza for similar reasons. Let's assume 10%. This gives us 8M pizza consumers in this segment.

Adding all of these up, we get 88M pizza consumers.

Interviewer: Does this number seem reasonable to you?

Candidate: I have assumed that the US has 320M people. I calculated that 88M people eat pizza, which would mean roughly a little more 25% of the population eats pizza. This number seems reasonable to me, what do you think?

Interviewer: I agree that the number seems reasonable, perhaps a little on the low side. Let's say that 90M people eat pizza to make the math a bit simpler.

Candidate: Great. Next, I need to estimate the frequency at which these 90M people eat pizza. Based on my personal experiences eating pizza, people will consume 2-3 slices or a quarter of a pizza, every meal. Let's say that they eat pizza once a week, which would give us roughly 52 meals times a quarter of a pizza each meal, or 13 pizzas a year.
Multiplying 13 pizzas a year with 90M people gives us 1.17B pizzas.

Interviewer: Let's say 1.2B pizzas consumed a year, and let's assume the average pizza costs $15.

Candidate: Great. So, 1.2B pizzas times $15 gives us a market size of $18B. In order to determine if this is a large market size, I'd like to compare it to the burger market size. Do we have that information?

Interviewer: Let's say that the burger market size is $30B.

Candidate: Wow. That means that the pizza market is much smaller than the burger market, about 60% of its size. My preliminary conclusion is that we should not enter the pizza market since it is a relatively small market. To further validate this, I'd like to compare the average profit margin in the burger market with that of the pizza market. Do we have that information?

Interviewer: Let's say that profit margins in the burger market are 3% and profit margins in the pizza market are 9%.

Candidate: This changes my conclusion. Although the pizza market is only 60% the size of the burger market, the profit margins are three times that of the burger market. Therefore, I think that the pizza market would be an attractive market to enter.

Interviewer: I agree with your interpretation of this data. What if I told you that the leading pizza restaurant in the city that Burger Guys is in has 10% market share. What conclusions can you draw?

Candidate: If the market leader has 10% market share, that implies that the market is fairly fragmented. This means that there are low barriers to entry.

Interviewer: What are some examples of barriers to entry that you can think of?

Candidate: We can think of barriers to entry as both economic barriers to entry and non-economic barriers to entry. Examples of economic barriers to entry would be: the capital required to start a pizza restaurant, economies of scale to have cost advantages, and distribution channels and infrastructure needed for pizza delivery. Examples of non-economic barriers to entry include: brand name in the pizza market, knowledge/expertise to make superior pizza, and restaurant differentiation from the other pizza restaurants in the market.

Interviewer: Let's say that the CEO walks in and wants an update and preliminary recommendation on what you have been working on so far. What do you say?

Candidate: Burger Guys has been experiencing a decline in profits because the quantity of burgers sold has decreased. This is caused by a change in customer preference towards consuming pizza. To address this, I recommend that we enter into the pizza market for the following three reasons.

One, customer food preferences are shifting from burgers to pizza. Our recent survey found that eating preferences for burgers has declined from 48% to 45% in the past year, while eating preferences for pizzas has increased from 28% to 35%.

Two, the pizza market is more attractive than the burger market. Although the pizza market is only $18B, 60% of the size of the burger market, the average profit margins are three times that of the burger market, 9% compared to 3%.

Three, the market is fairly fragmented, with the top player only having 10% of the market share. This implies that there are low barriers to entry for Burger Guys to enter the market.

For these three reasons, I recommend that we consider entering the pizza market. For next steps, I'd like to look into two things. One, I'd like to look at Burger Guys' capabilities to determine if we are capable of entering the pizza market. This would include looking into synergies between running a fast food burger restaurant and a pizza restaurant. Two, I'd like to do a revenue and cost analysis to determine if we would be profitable if we entered the pizza market.

Interviewer: Great, thanks. That concludes the case interview.

II. Understanding the Case Background Information

The case begins with the interviewer giving you the case background information and objective.

Some cases may have a very small amount of background information. In this instance, every single thing that the interviewer says may be important. Other cases may have a large amount of background information that will require you to make a judgement call on which pieces of information are important and which pieces are less important.

The main objectives for you are to:

1. Understand the situation of the case

2. Determine what the goals or objectives of the case are

3. Ask clarifying questions

During this part of the case interview, the interviewer is not specifically evaluating you on a certain set of criteria since the interviewer will be doing most of the talking. However, you are still leaving an impression on the interviewer based on the questions you ask. Therefore, ensure that you are:

- NOT asking irrelevant questions about the case

- NOT asking the interviewer to repeat a tremendous amount of information

- NOT interrupting the interviewer too much

The first objective, understanding the situation, requires that you have an understanding of the various pieces of information that the interviewer discloses to you. Examples of information that are likely important include:

- What is the name of the company/client that we are trying to help?

- What do they do or make?

- How are they doing in the market?

- What major actions has the company/client done recently?

- How is the market that they are in doing?

- What is the competitive landscape like?

- What have competitors been doing?

The second objective, determining the goals of the case, dictates what you will be doing for the rest of the case interview. Cases may have a single objective or multiple ones. Examples of common objectives are:

- Determine whether or not the company/client should enter a new market

- Determine whether or not the company/client should acquire another company

- Determine why the company/client is losing revenue

- Determine why the company/client has been experiencing increasing costs

- Determine why the profitability of the company/client has been decreasing

- Determine what to do about a new competitor entering the market

The third objective requires that you ask clarifying questions when needed. There may be a particular term that you are not familiar with, or you may need the interviewer to repeat a piece of information.

One question that comes up when I am giving mock interviews is whether or not it is okay to interrupt the interviewer with questions when they are giving you the case background information. My short answer to that question is that if it is an important question that will hinder your understanding for the rest of the case background information, go ahead and politely interrupt the interviewer to ask your question. It is better to ask the interviewer to repeat or explain one thing, rather than having to repeat the entire case background information because you did not understand a term or concept.

For example, suppose the case interview is about purchasing a timeshare company, but you have no idea what a timeshare is. If you don't know what timeshares are, it will be difficult for you to understand the rest of the case background. Therefore, it is in your best interest to understand what timeshares are right away, so that you can better absorb the information that follows.

For questions that will not hinder your understanding for the rest of the case background information, you should be able to hold off on asking those until the interviewer has finished speaking. Once they have finished talking, you can then ask your clarifying questions or ask them to repeat a thing or two.

Examples of clarifying questions include:

- Did you say that profits have gone down or revenue has gone down?

- You mentioned that the company sold four different items. What was the fourth one again?

- I'm not quite familiar with the term "share of wallet." What does that mean?

- Is our company based only in the US? Or are they global?

Very little evaluation occurs during this part of the case, as the interviewer is simply presenting you the case background information. As long as you don't ask irrelevant questions, ask the interviewer to repeat too much information, or interrupt the interviewer too frequently, you will be just fine.

Taking notes during the case interview

During this part of the case interview, you should be taking notes on what the interviewer is telling you.

I recommend orienting your sheet of paper so that it is landscape (long side on the bottom). Draw a vertical straight line on the page so that the left-hand side is roughly one-third of the page and the right-hand side is roughly two-thirds of the page. From this point on, use the left-hand side to take notes for the rest of the case. The right-hand side will have your framework that you will structure later on.

Any calculations or math that you do should be done on a separate sheet of paper. This way, you do not mix calculations with your framework or notes. As the case goes on, if there are any key takeaways or important pieces of information that you discover, make a note of it in your notes column. Doing this will make the conclusion part of the case interview much easier for you, as you have recorded all of the key pieces of information in one place.

You are most likely not going to be able to write down every single thing that your interviewer says. Therefore, it is important that you are taking notes in a bullet point format. You should not be taking notes in complete sentences. Feel free to use any shorthand notation, as long as you can easily recall what you mean later on in the case. An example of shorthand could be writing down "R$\downarrow$, C$\uparrow$" instead of "revenue has decreased and costs have increased."

You should be capturing all of the important information your interviewer is giving you and leaving out minor details that you could ask for later on in the case if needed.

III. Verifying Objectives

You've taken some great notes, and if you had any clarifying questions, you have asked them and had them answered. For this next part of the case interview, your objectives are to:

1. Synthesize and present the key pieces of information in a clear, concise, and confident way

2. Verify what the goals or objectives of the case are

This is the part of the case interview where your evaluation begins. In this part, the interviewer is looking for your:

- Ability to synthesize information and identify what is important

- Ability to communicate in a clear, concise, and confident way

For the first objective, synthesizing key pieces of information, you can differentiate yourself from other candidates if your recap of the information is short and sweet.

The most common mistake I see is people reciting back all of the information they have heard to the interviewer. The interviewer does not want to listen to an exact playback of what they have just said to the candidate. They are testing whether the interviewee can parse out the most important pieces of information from the rest of the minor details.

Another common mistake I see is interviewees inserting their own assumptions or conclusions during the recap. The recap should be strictly factual. You should not be inserting information that the interviewer has not given you. You can state your assumptions or conclusions in later parts of the case.

Example: Let's say that your interviewer gives you the following information:

Our client makes several varieties of sweet jams, such as strawberry, blueberry, and raspberry, in the US. During the past winter, a strong blizzard has hit one of the groves where the berries grow. As a result, our client has lost roughly a quarter of their berries. Because of this, they are considering planting peanuts in Mexico so that they can produce peanut butter in addition to sweet jams. This way, if a strong blizzard hits the US again, our client will still have peanuts to produce peanut butter. Should they enter the peanut butter market?

A bad recap:

> "Our client makes several varieties of sweet jams, such as strawberry, blueberry, and raspberry. During the past winter, a strong blizzard hit one of the groves where the berries grow. Our client lost roughly a quarter of their berries that they use for jams. Since this probably caused a decrease in profits, they are also considering planting peanuts in a different region to produce peanut butter. The objective is to determine whether or not they should enter the peanut butter market to increase profits."

This recap is bad for a variety of reasons. First, it is not concise. It is almost as long as the original statement given by the interviewer. Second, even though the recap is long, it leaves out important pieces of information (e.g. the client is a US company looking to expand internationally into Mexico). Third, the recap introduces some assumptions or conclusions that the interviewer never mentioned (e.g. decline in profits as a result of the blizzard).

A good recap:

> "Our client produces jams in the US. During the past winter, they have lost a quarter of their berries due to a blizzard. Because of this, they are considering planting peanuts in Mexico and entering the peanut butter market. The objective is to determine whether or not they should enter the peanut butter market."

This recap is much more concise than the previous one. All of the important pieces of information are captured, and no assumptions/conclusions are inserted. The recap is strictly factual.

For the second objective, verifying the goals of the case, it is important to make sure that you and the interviewer are aligned on what the goals of the case are. If you and the interviewer have different ideas of what the objectives are, you will be wasting a lot of time during the interview asking questions that are not relevant or doing analysis that is not important to developing a recommendation. It will be very difficult for you to recover from this misalignment. Even the best interview candidates in the world will still verify the objectives with the interviewer because they know how important it is.

Although this part of the case is simple, it is important to do this part well. What you say during this part of the case interview sets the tone for what the interviewer is to expect from you in later parts. Secondly, if this part of the case interview goes smoothly, you will feel much more confident and comfortable with the rest of the case moving forward. You can easily build up momentum and confidence by doing this part well since this part is not technical or difficult.

IV. Developing a Structured Framework

Developing a structured framework is by far the most difficult part of the case interview. If you nail down this part, the rest of the case interview will come much easier to you. Conversely, a weak framework can set you up to crash and burn later on in the case interview.

The good news is that you are not expected to come up with a framework instantaneously. Generally, you are allowed to ask for a few minutes to gather and structure your thoughts to develop a framework.

What is a framework? At a high level, a framework is an organized and structured set of ideas that you can explore and learn more about in order to help discover the answer and deliver on the objective of the case. The broad ideas in the framework are referred to as "buckets." For the rest of this book, I will use this term. You should also use the term "buckets," as you will sound more like a consultant.

The most generic framework that candidates commonly use is a four-bucket framework consisting of: customer, competition, product, and company. For example, if the objective of one case interview is to determine whether or not a company should enter a new market, we can use this four-bucket framework to gather information that will help us develop and strengthen a recommendation.

While this framework is useful, we can do better than that. The framework listed above will not help differentiate yourself from the other candidates. It is extremely generic and overused.

Criteria for developing an exceptional framework

Before I present my strategy for developing frameworks, let's review all of the criteria the case interviewer is looking for in an exceptional framework:

1. All buckets must be relevant to the objective of the case

2. Buckets should not have any overlap with each another

3. There should be three to four buckets (however, some cases may naturally have only two)

4. The framework is not a generic framework (like the one listed above)

5. Under each bucket, there are two to three sub-bullets, which add detail and specifics about what each bucket means

6. The sub-bullets are all relevant to the objective of the case

7. The sub-bullets do not have any overlap with one another

Looking at the first objective, all buckets should be relevant to the objective of the case. One common mistake I see among candidates is that they come in with pre-memorized frameworks. As is often the case with pre-memorized frameworks, not all of the buckets or sub-bullets will be relevant to the objective of the case. Presenting a framework in which not all of the buckets are relevant allows the interviewer to quickly figure out that you are just leveraging memorized frameworks and are not truly thinking about the problem. This is a huge pitfall for the vast majority of candidates.

Example: Let's say that you are given a case on whether or not Company A should acquire Company B. If you used the generic framework: customer, competition, product, and company, several of these buckets aren't relevant. For example, is looking at the products of Company A and Company B the most important thing to look into? The answer is no. This framework is missing key topics such as synergies, cost of acquisition, and the attractiveness of the market Company B is in.

For the second objective, the buckets should not overlap with each other. What I mean by this is that each bucket must be distinct from all of the other buckets. Buckets that are not distinct and have overlap with one another show poor structural and organizational thinking. Structure is a very important characteristic that interviewers look for.

Example: If two of my buckets are "cost" and "financial considerations," then the buckets are not distinct from one another. One component of "financial considerations" is cost, which I have as another bucket. The two buckets overlap, and show a messy organization of ideas.

For the third objective, coming up with only one or two buckets may show that you are not very good at brainstorming ideas. Therefore, you should aim to have a minimum of three buckets. On the flipside, having eight buckets will not earn you extra points with the interviewer. More likely than not, if you have eight buckets, a few of your buckets will not be distinct from one another and overlap. Again, this shows poor structure. The sweet spot is usually three to four buckets.

I do want to note that there are some case interviews where two buckets should naturally be used. For example, if the interviewer asks for the benefits and costs of starting an NBA basketball team, your buckets should naturally be some version of the words "benefits" and "costs." However, just because you are using two buckets does not mean you cannot further structure and subdivide these. You can split "benefits" into "long-term benefits" and "short-term benefits." You can split "costs" into "economic costs" and "non-economic costs."

For the fourth objective, this is the number one mistake that I see with candidates. The biggest takeaway in this book is to use a unique framework for each case you are given, NOT a generic one. I will go over how to do this later on in this chapter.

Candidates come into a case interview having read one or two popular case interview books. And so, for whatever case they are given, the framework buckets that they use are some combination of: customer, competition, product, and company. Again, most candidates are using some variation of this framework. You are not helping yourself stand out from the rest of the crowd if you use this framework as well.

For the fifth objective, you should elaborate on what your buckets mean by adding two to three sub-bullets under each bucket that you have. For example, just having a bucket of "market" would not be very interesting on its own. To add detail about what you mean, you can add sub-bullets such as "market size," "market growth rate," and "average profit margins in the market." The sub-bullets specify exactly what pieces of information you want to discuss or learn more about within a bucket.

For the sixth and seventh objectives, just as your buckets had to be relevant to the objective of the case and not overlap with one another, so too do all of your sub-bullets under each bucket.

Looking at the requirements above, it may appear difficult to you to come up with a perfect framework for each case that you get. Given the time pressure of only having a few minutes to come up with a framework, the task is daunting for the majority of candidates.

Memorizing frameworks beforehand will help you come up with a framework more easily, but those frameworks may not be entirely relevant to the objective of the case and may be generic. On the flipside, coming up with a unique framework from scratch each time would ensure that the framework is relevant to the objective of the case and be unique, but this is challenging to do in only a few minutes. What is the solution to this dilemma?

Strategy to tackling frameworks

My solution is a strategy that is somewhere in between these two approaches. There are definitely things that you must memorize and be able to recall from the top of your head, but you also get to do novel, creative thinking throughout the process.

The strategy I recommend for tackling frameworks sounds simple, but will take time and practice to fully develop and master. Memorize a list of eight different buckets. When you encounter a case:

Step One: Mentally run through the list of eight buckets and select the three to four that are the most relevant.

Step Two: Once you select the buckets, brainstorm two to three sub-bullets for each of the buckets.

That's it. You only need to memorize eight things.

For step one, you should have these eight buckets fully memorized by heart. You should be able to wake up in the middle of the night and immediately recall the eight buckets within ten seconds. This part is fairly easy.

For step two, this is where you will need to do most of your thinking and spend the majority of your time mastering the skill. The two to three sub-bullets should be tailored to the exact case that you are trying to solve for. They should not be completely memorized. Why? Because sub-bullets that are relevant for one case may not be relevant for other cases. How exactly do we come up with these sub-bullets? The simple answer is that as you do more and more cases, the sub-bullets will come easier to you as you are brainstorming and thinking about them.

What are the eight buckets that you need to memorize? They are as follows:

1. Market attractiveness

2. Competitive landscape

3. Company attractiveness OR company capabilities

4. Customer segmentation and needs

5. Financial considerations

6. Risks and mitigations

7. Synergies

8. Create your own bucket

First of all, the names of the buckets are longer than one word. Instead of using the bucket "market," we use "market attractiveness." Instead of "competition," we use "competitive landscape." Although these are common buckets used in frameworks, we create the illusion of a more unique framework by adding a slightly longer description to the bucket name.

Second, do not be tied to the exact wording of the bucket names. For example, look at the third bullet above. If in a case you are looking into acquiring another company, "company attractiveness" would be the right bucket name to use. If in another case, you are looking into entering a market, "company capabilities" would be the right bucket name to use. You may slightly customize the naming of the buckets for each case. If you are analyzing the cellphone market, you could call the bucket "cellphone market attractiveness" instead of "market attractiveness." If you are analyzing a company named Diamond Co., you can call the bucket "Diamond Co. capabilities" instead of "company capabilities." What is important is that you are memorizing the concept of each bucket. Do not be so tied down to memorizing the exact phrases or words as long as you remember the concept or theme behind each bucket.

Understanding the eight buckets

Below, I have provided a description of each of the eight buckets. The descriptions for each bucket are meant to give you an idea of what possible sub-bullets could be. Remember that you do not need to memorize sub-bullets, only the general names of the eight buckets. When you get a new case, you will first select the three to four buckets from your list of eight that are the most relevant. Then, you will naturally think of the sub-bullets, depending on the context of the case. This is where you have the opportunity to do your own creative thinking. To develop these sub-bullets, you just need to be very familiar and comfortable with what each of the buckets mean.

1. Market attractiveness: Anything about the market goes into this bucket. What is the market size? What is the market growth rate? What are average profit margins in the market? What are the major trends/changes going on in the market? Are there new technologies in the market? Are there new regulations? Is the market developing or mature? Is the market converging with another market?

2. Competitive landscape: Anything about competitors goes into this bucket. Who are the competitors in the market? How much market share does each player have? What products do competitors sell? What capabilities do competitors have? What do some competitors do to differentiate themselves from the other players in the market? What are the barriers to entry?

3. Company attractiveness/company capabilities: Anything about the company you are working with or the company that you are looking to analyze or acquire goes into this bucket. What line of products does the company offer? What ways do the products differentiate themselves from other products? How much market share does the company have? How profitable is the company? What distribution channels does the company have? What partnerships does the company have? How much buying power does the company have? What is the go-to-market strategy of the company? In what geographic regions is the company based in? Is the company growing or declining?

4. Customer segmentation and needs: Anything about customers in the target market goes into this bucket. What are the different customer segments? What are the characteristics of each customer segment? What are the needs/preferences of each customer segment? How are customers changing in each customer segment? How profitable is each customer segment?

5. Financial considerations: Anything regarding revenue, costs, and profit goes into this bucket. Is the implication of this business decision profitable? What are the different revenue elements? What are the different cost elements? How can we increase revenues? How can we decrease costs? What is the pricing strategy? How long will it take to breakeven? What is the cost of acquisition? What is the financial exit-strategy of this business decision?

6. Synergies: Anything about synergies between two companies, or two products goes into this bucket. What are the possible revenue synergies? What are the possible cost synergies? Are synergies realizable? How long will realizing these synergies take?

7. Risks and mitigations: This is a versatile bucket that you can use in frameworks where you need one more bucket but can't think of one. What are the risks of this business decision? What is the likely impact of such risks? Can these risks be mitigated?

8. Create your own bucket: This eighth bucket gives you the creativity and flexibility to create your own bucket. Sometimes during a case, there will be a bucket that comes to mind that is highly relevant to the case, but may not be explicitly captured by the seven buckets above. Feel free to create your own bucket for cases as long as the bucket follows the criteria of an exceptional framework that was outlined earlier in this chapter.

Advantages of this framework strategy

What is the advantage of this framework strategy over all of the other strategies out there?

First of all, with every case that you do, you are guaranteed to come up with a custom and unique framework. You will not be using a single generic framework that all of the other candidates have memorized. It is a custom framework because you are choosing a new combination of three to four buckets from the list of eight for every case that you get. Granted, if you do two market entry cases, your frameworks might be the same, but your framework for market entry will be different from a merger and acquisition case, a new product launch case, a pricing case, etc.

The framework you develop will also be unique in that no other candidate out there will be using the same framework that you are. Why? Because for each bucket you are creatively brainstorming two to three sub-bullets that are specific to the case that you are solving for. By leveraging this strategy, you instantly differentiate yourself from the thousands of other candidates out there, the majority of whom will be solving a case with a generic framework that they memorized from another case interview book.

Secondly, this strategy is implementable. What do I mean by this? Some other case interview books out there might tell you what framework to memorize for every case scenario. If there are 15 different case scenarios, you'll need to memorize 15 different frameworks. Not only will your framework be generic and likely not entirely relevant to the case objective, but very few people can memorize 15 different frameworks. What if I told you that you only had to memorize eight things? It is definitely more implementable than memorizing 15 frameworks.

Thirdly, this strategy guarantees that you will not go blank during the moment of silence when you brainstorm and structure your framework. If you know your list of eight buckets by heart, you have nothing to worry about when brainstorming your framework. In the worst-case scenario, you can pick a few buckets that you think are relevant to the case and go with those. You will never have a blank sheet of paper to work with.

Examples of this strategy put to use

I have included some sample frameworks below that I developed for common types of case interviews to give you some ideas for how you can put this framework strategy to use. Again, you do not need to memorize the frameworks below. You only need to memorize the eight buckets described above and know how to use this framework strategy.

Example 1: Market Entry Case – Should Company A enter Market X?

- Market attractiveness
    - What is the market size?
    - What is the market growth rate?
    - What are average profit margins in the market?

- Company A capabilities
    - What capabilities can Company A leverage to enter Market X?
    - Does Company A have any experience related to Market X?
    - Is Company A able to handle the risks involved in entering the new market?

- Financial considerations
    - Will entering Market X be profitable?
    - How long will it take to break even?

- Competitive landscape of Market X
    - Is the competitive landscape fragmented or concentrated?
    - Do competitors in Market X have differentiated capabilities or products?
    - What are the barriers to entry?

Example 2: Profitability Case – What is causing Company A to lose profits? What can be done to address this issue?

- Financial considerations
    - How have revenues changed for Company A?
        - Quantity
        - Price
    - How have costs changed for Company A?
        - Variable costs
        - Fixed costs

- Competitive landscape
    - Have competitors done anything differently?
    - Have new competitors entered the market?

- o Have competitors also lost profits?

- Customer segmentation and needs
    - o Have customer needs or preferences changed?
    - o Have customer purchasing behaviors changed?
    - o Has the number of customers decreased?

- Market trends
    - o Are there any new technologies affecting the market?
    - o Are there any new regulations affecting the market?
    - o What other major trends are occurring in the market?

Example 3: Merger & Acquisition Case – Should Company A acquire Company B?

- Attractiveness of Company B
    - o How profitable is Company B?
    - o Does Company B have any differentiated capabilities or products?
    - o What is the brand name of Company B like?

- Attractiveness of the market Company B is in
    - o What is the market size?
    - o What is the market growth rate?
    - o What are the average profit margins in the market?

- Synergies
    - o What revenue synergies can be realized from the acquisition?
    - o What cost synergies can be realized from the acquisition?
    - o Are these synergies realizable?

- Financial considerations
    - o Is the acquisition of Company B at a fair price?
    - o How long will it take to break even?
    - o What are the possible exit strategies for acquiring Company B?

What if I developed a framework different from the examples above?

For a given case, there could be a chance that six or more of the buckets are relevant to the case. How do you pick just three to four buckets from these? The short answer is that you should pick the three to four that are the most relevant to the case. In other words, select the buckets that you think will give you the highest chance of cracking the case.

Let's say that for a given case, I select the following three buckets: market attractiveness, company attractiveness, and financial considerations. But you select market attractiveness, company attractiveness, and competitive landscape. Which framework is better? As long as the buckets are highly relevant to the case, different frameworks can be used to solve the same case. That is the beauty of this strategy. Each person using it will come up with a unique framework.

V. Handling the Moment of Silence

Before you present your structured framework, there will be a few minutes of silence when neither the interviewer nor you will be talking. There are a few points here worth discussing.

The objectives of this part of the case are:

1. Do not take more than two to three minutes of complete silence

2. Keep track of how much time has gone by

3. If you are approaching two to three minutes and need more time, connect with the interviewer to let them know you need another minute

There is nothing that the interviewer is explicitly evaluating you on in this part of the case since there will be mainly silence. However, the interviewer is still observing your demeanor and behavior. To ensure that the interviewer does not form a negative impression of you, make sure you are:

- NOT spending more than two to three minutes in complete silence

- NOT visibly looking stressed or frantic

This is the only part of the case interview when it is okay for there to be complete silence between you and the interviewer. For all other parts of the case, the interview should be collaborative and you and the interviewer should be talking back and forth in discussion.

If you do not achieve the first objective, not taking more than two to three minutes of silence, this can make the interviewer uncomfortable. They could get worried that they will not be able to get through the entire case with you. Interviewers will generally try to get through the entire case with a candidate, even if the candidate performs poorly. This makes the interview experience better for both parties. I recommend that you practice developing your framework for case interviews so that you can finish in under two to three minutes comfortably.

For the second objective, how can you tell how much time has gone by? The first method is practice. When you are doing mock case interviews with your case partner, have them time how long it takes you to develop your framework. From this feedback, you should eventually be able to build in an "internal clock" so that you know roughly how long one minute, two minutes, and three minutes feel like. It is important to do this beforehand because in a high-pressure situation like a case interview, time can pass slowly or quickly, depending on how you are feeling.

An alternative method is to subtlety glance at your watch (if you are wearing one). The only downside is that if the interviewer catches you looking at your watch, it may make them feel like you are in a rush to go somewhere. So, try not to make looking at your watch too obvious.

For the third objective, if you feel that you are going over three minutes and notice the interviewer getting restless and impatient, you can do this one trick. Simply break the silence by saying something like "I am just wrapping up now; I will need another 30 seconds" or "Thanks for your patience; I just need another minute or so." This may alleviate the awkwardness that comes with long periods of silence. You can also make yourself sound confident as you are saying these things since it shows you are proactively monitoring your progress and the time.

VI. Presenting Your Framework

Structuring your framework is the hard part; presenting it is the easy part. For this part of the case interview, make sure that you:

1. Turn the paper around to face the interviewer so that they can read your framework

2. Walk your interviewer through your framework at a high-level

3. Check in with the interviewer so that they are aligned with your framework

During this part, the interviewer is looking for:

- A structured, relevant, and unique framework (see IV. Developing a Structured Framework)

- The ability to communicate in a clear, concise, and confident way

For the first objective, I recommend that you physically turn your paper around so that the interviewer is looking at your framework. This will make it easier for your interviewer to understand how you are thinking about the problem because they will be both reading it and hearing it. However, this is not always possible, depending on how the seating arrangement is set up.

For the second objective, walking your interviewer through your framework, state how many areas you'd like to look into and then list what the names of your buckets are. Then for each bucket, spend 30 seconds discussing the most important sub-bullets of each.

For the third objective, it is important to check in with the interviewer to see if they are aligned with the framework and your approach to the problem. Say something like "Does this sound good?" or "Does that make sense?" As a reminder, you want to touch base with the interviewer throughout the entire case interview process so that you are on the right track.

Below is an example of how you should sound when you are presenting your framework. For this example, let's say that you are given a case on whether or not a US strawberry jam producer should enter the peanut butter market. You should present your framework in the following way:

> "To determine whether or not it is a good idea to enter the peanut butter market, there are four areas I'd like to look into.
>
> First, I'd like to look at the market attractiveness of the peanut butter market. I'd like to look into what the market size is, what the market growth rate is, and what the average margins are in the peanut butter market. Essentially, I want to know: is this market attractive enough for us to enter?
>
> Second, I'd like to look at the competitive landscape. How many competitors are in the market? How much share do they have? I want to figure out if the market is concentrated or fragmented, and what the barriers to entry are. By looking at this category, we can better understand how difficult it would be to enter.
>
> Third, I'd like to look at our own company capabilities. Do we have the ability to create a great peanut butter product? Do we have any expertise in the area and know how to grow peanuts? Do we know what the recipe for peanut butter should be? Can we leverage our existing jam production equipment? Or do we need to purchase new equipment entirely? Can we leverage our existing customer and distribution channels to sell peanut butter successfully?
>
> For the fourth and final area, I'd like to look into the financial considerations of entering the market. Will we be profitable by selling peanut butter? How long will it take for us to

break even from the initial investment we put in? What is management's financial goals for entering the peanut butter market, and can these goals be achieved? To do this, we can project what revenues will be, and estimate what costs will be to figure out what the profitability would look like.

Does this sound good?"

When you finish presenting your framework, the interviewer should know exactly what the different buckets or areas that you want to look into are. After this, you and the interviewer will begin solving the case together.

VII. Starting the Case

Once you are finished presenting your framework, this is when solving the case starts. All case interviews can be classified into one of two types:

1. Cases that the interviewer leads

2. Cases that you lead

If the case is led by the interviewer, you will not be doing much talking during this part of the case. If the case is led by you, then there are a few things that the interviewer is looking for during this part:

- The ability to identify a high priority area to start the case

- The ability to communicate in a clear, concise, and confident way

I would estimate that most case interviews are led by the interviewer, but there are some that you will lead. Some cases may have a mix of the two, with you leading parts of the case, and the interviewer leading other parts. It does not matter which type of case interview you are given, the approach and methodology is exactly the same.

Cases that the interviewer leads

For the first type of case, you will know if the case is led by the interviewer because once you've presented your framework, the interviewer effectively "takes over." They will start you down a path of analysis, or will ask you a question that you will both then discuss. When you have completed that analysis or question, the interviewer will guide or steer you towards the next analysis or question. This will continue until the end of the case, when the interviewer asks you for a recommendation that synthesizes everything that you have learned so far.

After you present your framework, the interviewer might say something like this: "That framework sounds great. Let's start off by estimating the market size. How would you approach determining the size of the peanut butter market in the US?" This type of dialogue is a clear indication of a case interview in which the interviewer leads.

Cases that you lead

The second type of case interviews are the ones in which you are expected to lead. These are a little bit more work. You may be "leading" the case, but you still must get approval or confirmation from the interviewer before doing any analysis or discussion in one specific area. In this sense, the interviewer is still ultimately controlling which direction the case is going. The interviewer is now just taking a slightly more passive role than in a case interview that the interviewer leads.

Remember that you are collaborating with the interviewer. The case interview should be a discussion with both parties talking, no matter if the interviewer is leading the case or if you are leading the case. The main difference with the latter is that once you've presented your framework, your interviewer will ask where you want to start.

When asked this, state in which area of your framework you'd like to start and why. There is no wrong answer here as there is no way for you to know which areas will have the key pieces of information for solving the case. As long as you state where you'd like to start and the reasoning behind it makes sense, you will be fine. If you pick an area that the interviewer does not want to go down, they will suggest an alternative area.

The most important part of solving a case that you are leading is to check in frequently with the interviewer to make sure you are going down the correct path.

Example: After you present your framework, the interviewer might say something like this: "That framework sounds great. Where should we start?"

You could say something like:

> "I think we should start off by looking at the competitive landscape. I want to figure out how concentrated or fragmented the market is in order to determine how difficult it would be to enter. We could also look into what the barriers to entry are, and if they can be met. Does that sound good?"

If that is an area that the interviewer wants you to look into, the interviewer would say something like "That sounds good. Let's look more into the competitive landscape."

Conversely, if that is an area that the interviewer does not want you to look into, the interviewer would say something like "While I agree that looking at the competitive landscape makes sense, we don't have much information in that area. Why don't we start by sizing the peanut butter market instead?" The interviewer could also ask you to propose another area to start solving and answering the case.

Similarities between the two types of case interviews

For either type of case interview, if during any part of the case the interviewer does not lead you where to go next, you should suggest the next step or next area to move towards. Again, it does not matter what area you suggest as long as it is a logical next step and helps solve or answer the overall case objective. If it happens to be an area that the interviewer wants you to drill down into, then the interviewer will let you proceed with the suggested area. If it is not what the interviewer had in mind, then the interviewer will step in and guide you towards the area that they want you to go down.

In this sense, both of the two types of case interviews are exactly the same. The interviewer is ultimately guiding you in both scenarios. It is just a matter of whether or not the interviewer is blatantly telling you which area to look into or you are deciding which area to look into with approval and input from the interviewer. Just make sure that you are prepared for both.

VIII. Solving Quantitative Problems

The majority of the quantitative work in a case interview will come in either the form of market sizing or breakeven analysis. There may be smaller quantitative questions asked, but if you can solve market sizing and breakeven problems with ease, all quantitative questions should be no problem for you.

This is what the interviewer is looking for:

- General problem solving capabilities

- Ability to provide structure to quantitative problems

- Comfort in working with numbers; the ability to easily execute basic mathematical computations (e.g. don't make a lot of math mistakes)

- Ability to communicate in a clear, concise, and confident way

For people that are earning or have earned a quantitative or engineering degree, this part of the case will be the easiest for you. For others, this part could be more challenging for you if you have not done math in a while.

Whichever is the case, you only need to know how to do very basic math. You need to know how to add, subtract, multiply, and divide. You also need to know how to deal with percentages, fractions, ratios and how to convert from one to another. Other than these things, you really don't need to know any more math beyond that. You don't need to know calculus, statistics, or more advanced math.

Sounds easy right? Given the high pressure situation of a case interview, even the most mathematically competent candidates get nervous during these exercises and can easily make an arithmetic mistake here and there. Therefore, it is important to consistently check your work throughout long computations to ensure that you have not made any mistakes.

Market sizing

The first type of quantitative problem solving is market sizing. In simple terms, market sizing is an exercise in which you make assumptions to calculate how large a market is.

Unless something else is specified, market size has the units of dollars ($), or whatever other currency is being used, spent in one year. Other versions of market sizing may ask you to estimate the number of units sold, rather than estimate the monetary value of the units.

Most of the time, market sizing is asked for just the US. However, other times you might get asked for the global market size, so be sure to specify which one you should be calculating with the interviewer.

Examples of market sizing: (note that the units for these should be in dollars spent in one year):

- What is the size of the contact lens market?

- How much money is spent on computers every year?

- What is the market size of wine?

Some other examples: (note that these units are not dollars spent in one year):

- How many cars are sold in the US every year?

- How many gallons of gas do Americans use every year?

- How many minutes do Americans spend talking on their phones every year?

These market sizing questions might seem tough to answer immediately, but with enough practice, market sizing becomes straight forward and repetitive.

At a high level, there are two different methods to tackle market sizing. You can either take a top-down approach or a bottom-up approach. A top-down approach is when you start with a very large number, and then refine/filter/drill-down until you get to the answer. A bottom-up approach is when you start with a small number, and then build/multiply it up until you get to the answer.

Let's say that we are asked to determine the market size of ice cream in the US.

For a top-down approach, start with the number of people in the US. Then, estimate what percentage of the US population eats ice cream. Next, figure out how many pints of ice cream the average ice cream consumer would eat in a week. From that, extrapolate how many pints of ice cream are consumed in a year. Finally, estimate the average price per pint of ice cream, and multiply everything together to get the market size.

For a bottom-up approach, start with a single ice cream store. Then, estimate how many people visit the store a day and how many pints of ice cream a person would purchase on average. Next, calculate how much money the ice cream store makes in one day, and extrapolate that to a year. Finally, estimate how many ice cream stores are in a city or town and then figure out how many cities or towns are in the US. Multiplying all of these things together gives you the market size of ice cream.

I strongly recommend going with a top-down approach because it is generally easier to work with. Why is it easier to work with? Looking at the example above, it is not that difficult to make up reasonable numbers for each assumption. You should know that the US is roughly 300M people (320M is another common estimate). You can estimate the percentage of people who eat ice cream by thinking about your friends and family and how many of them would eat ice cream. You can estimate how much a person eats by thinking about how much you would reasonably eat in a week. You can estimate the dollar ($) price per pint of ice cream from your experiences in a supermarket or ice cream parlor. In other words, all of these assumptions can be made up by you fairly easily because you can relate to them.

Now let's look at the bottom-up approach. It is a little bit more difficult to estimate how many people visit an ice cream store in one day. You could estimate how long it takes you to walk into an ice cream store, purchase ice cream, and then leave. You could then divide the number of hours of operation the ice cream store is open for to see how many customers the ice cream store can serve. But then again, the ice cream store will not always be completely busy, so you will have to scale down that number and assume that the ice cream store is only busy 50% of the time. The extremely difficult number to come up with is the number of cities/towns in the US. Why? This is typically not a number that people have in the back of their heads. Is it 1,000? Is it 10,000? Is it 100,000? Even deciding the order of magnitude for this assumption is difficult. For this reason, I recommend going with a top-down approach instead of a bottom-up approach. It is much easier to come up with numbers for the assumptions that you will need to make.

Almost all market sizing questions I've received can be solved with a top-down approach. However, if you feel that a bottom-up approach would be easier for a particular market sizing question, then go with that method. It does not matter which method you choose as long as the approach gets you to the answer in a simple, easy way.

Now that we have the general approach out of the way, let's discuss the process of solving a market sizing question.

One mistake that interviewers commonly make is jumping right into the math and calculations without taking much time to think about their holistic approach. If you are an expert market sizer, this is fine to do, but most of us need some time to process the question and come up with a structure for what approach we want to use.

Therefore, the first step in solving a market sizing problem is to ask the interviewer for some time to structure an approach. In almost all case interviews, the interviewer will give you the time to structure and frame your approach.

When developing your structure, avoid using numbers and avoid doing any calculations at all. Remember, you are developing the approach, or steps, that you are going to take to calculate the market size. We are not making up any numbers or doing any math calculations yet.

Let's take the example of "What is the size of the contact lens market in the US?" Using a top-down method, your approach should be something like this written on your piece of paper:

- The number of people in the US

- Segmenting the number of people in the US by age

- Estimating the percentage of each age group that has vision problems

- Estimating the percentage of people with vision problems in each age group that wear contact lens (instead of glasses or laser eye surgery)

- Estimating the number of pairs of contact lenses one person wears a year

- Estimating the cost of a single pair of contact lenses

- Multiplying across all of these will give you the market size of contact lenses in the US

You would then share this approach with your interviewer and get their approval or input before beginning to do any mathematical calculations. You could say something like the following:

> "In order to size the contact lens market in the US, I will first start with the US population. I will then segment the US population by different age groups because different age

groups have different percentages of people that have vision problems.

Within each age group, I would estimate the percentage of people that have vision problems. Next, I would estimate what percentage of those folks wear contact lenses.

After that, I would estimate how many pairs of contact lenses the average person wears in a year. Then, I will estimate the price per pair of contact lens.

Finally, I can multiply all of these things together to get the market size of contact lenses in the US."

Again, notice that there are no numbers or math calculations done when structuring the approach.

Once you have written this out on your piece of paper (you don't need to write out so many words as I did since you will be talking over these points), communicate your approach with your interviewer. In most cases, the interviewer will say that the approach is fine, and you can start making assumptions and calculations. In other cases, the interviewer might make some comments to modify your approach so that it will be easier for you to calculate the final answer.

Either way, once you've set up the approach to solve the market sizing question, the rest is just doing simple arithmetic.

Let's continue our example and assume that the interviewer approves of our approach. In about half of all market sizing problems, you will be expected to make up the numbers for all of your assumptions. In the other half of market sizing problems, the interviewer will have some numbers already made up for you to use. To determine which scenario you fall under, you can simply ask your interviewer whether they have any data that you can use, or if you should make up numbers for your assumptions yourself.
Either way, when you are doing the math and performing the calculations, there should not be silence between you and the interviewer. You should be "doing math out loud" and walking the

interviewer through the calculations and assumptions. Also, you should try to justify the numbers that you make up for your assumptions. These numbers can be based on something that you read, your experience in life, or any other methodology that you've used to come up with the numbers.

Let's continue our example of solving for the contact lens market size in the US. You should say something like this as you are calculating the market size:

> "First, starting with the US population, let's assume that there are roughly 320M people in the US. To segment by age, I'm going to assume four age groups of (0-20), (20-40), (40-60), and (60-80). This means that there are 80M people in each of the four different age groups.
>
> I'll assume that 20% of the people in the first age group have vision problems. I chose only 20% because generally, I think that your vision is good while you are young, but will get worse with age. This means 16M (80M * 20%) people have vision problems in this age group.
>
> I'll assume that 30% of people in the second age group have vision problems. As people get older, there is a greater likelihood that they will have vision problems due to aging. Therefore, 24M (80M * 30%) people have vision problems in this group.
>
> I'll assume that 50% of people in the third and fourth groups have vision problems. Again, the rationale behind this is that vision tends to get worse with age. Therefore, 80M (160M * 50%) people have vision problems across these two age groups.
>
> Adding up the four groups, we get a total of 120M people with vision problems (16M + 24M + 80M). Based on thinking about who among my friends and family wear contact lenses instead of glasses, let's assume roughly a third wear contact lenses. That means 40M people wear contact lenses (120M * 1/3).

> Next, let's assume contact lenses are disposable, and 2 pairs are needed each month. This is based on the disposable contact lenses that I use. This means that one person would need 24 pairs a year (2 pairs * 12 months).
>
> Multiplying the 40M people who wear contact lenses with 24 pairs a year gives 960M pairs of contact lenses worn by people in a year.
>
> My contact lenses cost roughly $5 a pair. Therefore, the market size of contact lenses is $4.8B (960M pairs * $5 per pair). $4.8B is the market size for contact lenses in the US."

Again, notice how I am walking the interviewer through every step of the calculation. Even though it sounds painful, doing so will greatly reduce the chance that you make a mathematical mistake since you are doing the math out loud. It will also ensure that the interviewer is following along.

Secondly, notice that I am providing some justifications for my numbers. I am not making them up out of thin air, but trying to explain where and how I got those numbers.

One common concern among candidates is that their answer will be off by an order of magnitude or more. You should not worry about this because the interviewer does not care about whether or not you get the correct market size answer. If the correct answer is $4B, someone who got an answer of $5B will not be perceived as a better candidate than someone who got the answer of $10B. The interviewer is evaluating you on: (1) the structured approach that you developed in this market sizing exercise and (2) whether or not you did the math easily without making any major mistakes.

A second concern among candidates is whether they should spend time memorizing a bunch of different statistics that could help them with market sizing problems. This could be helpful, but is not worth investing too much of your energy or time on. There are only two statistics that you have to memorize:

- U.S. population is 300M or 320M (use whichever number is easier to do math with)

- World population is 7B

That is it. You can make up or estimate all of the other statistics or numbers that you may need for market sizing.

With that said, here are three market sizing questions that you can try on your own:

- How many cars are sold in the US every year?
- What is the market size of wine in the US?
- How much money does a typical football game bring in?

Breakeven analysis

The second type of quantitative question that you might get asked is a breakeven analysis. A breakeven analysis calculates what would have to be true in order for you to achieve exactly zero profits. This type of question is much easier than the market sizing question because you simply follow a standard mathematical equation that calculates the breakeven point.

Before we begin, let's take a look at three simple equations that you will need to know. For all of the equations below, I will bold the ones that you must memorize and know by heart.

Profit = Revenue – Costs

*Revenue = Quantity * Price*

*Costs = (Quantity * Variable Costs) + Fixed Costs*

If we insert the last two equations into the first one, we get the expanded formula for profit:

Profit = (Quantity * Price) – [(Quantity * Variable Costs) + Fixed Costs]

A breakeven analysis looks at the scenario in which profit = 0. Doing this with the profit equation above:

0 = (Quantity * Price) – [(Quantity * Variable Costs) + Fixed Costs]

Now, if we rearrange this equation, we can simplify it a bit to derive the breakeven equation.

Quantity * (Price – Variable Costs) = Fixed Costs

You can use either the profit equation or the breakeven equation to solve breakeven analysis problems. The first equation is the original profit equation while the latter equation is the slightly simplified version of the profit equation that already sets profit = 0. Notice how both of the equations have four different variables (remember profit = 0 in breakeven). In breakeven analysis, three of the variables will be given, and you will solve for the fourth.

For example, let's say that you are considering opening a pizza store for a national pizza chain. You would sell pizzas at $10 each. You estimate that the dough required to make a single pizza would cost $0.50, the cheese would cost $0.75, the tomato sauce would cost $0.75, and the toppings would cost $2.00 to make a single pizza. The rent that you pay for the building would be $100K/year. You would hire two employees at a salary of $75K/year per employee. Finally, you would have to pay $50K a year royalty to the national pizza chain that you are opening the store under for using their brand and recipe. Assuming that there are no other costs, how many pizzas would you need to sell in order to break even?

Price = $10/pizza

Variable Costs = $0.50 (dough) + $0.75 (cheese) + $0.75 (tomato sauce) + $2.00 (toppings)

Variable Costs = $4.00/pizza

Fixed Costs = $100K (rent) + [2 * $75K] (two employees) + $50K (royalties)

Fixed Costs = $300K

Using the profit equation:

Profit = (Quantity * Price) − [(Quantity * Variable Costs) + Fixed Costs]

$0 = 10Q - (4Q + 300{,}000)$

$0 = 10Q - 4Q - 300{,}000$

$6Q = 300{,}000$

Q = 50,000

You would need to sell 50,000 pizzas to break even.

Using the breakeven equation also yields the same answer, but with one less step.

Quantity * (Price − Variable Costs) = Fixed Costs

$Q * (10 - 4) = 300{,}000$

$6Q = 300{,}000$

Q = 50,000

We get the same answer. You would need to sell 50,000 pizzas to break even.

Now that you know how to solve market sizing and breakeven analysis problems, you are ready to solve any quantitative problem that gets thrown your way in a case interview.

Minimizing mistakes while doing math

It is very important to make no math mistakes during a case interview. Remember, the interviewer is assessing your comfort in working with numbers, and whether you have the ability to execute basic mathematical computations with ease. You want to give off the perception that math is easy and effortless for you. You may be able to get away with a single miscalculation, but several math mistakes reflect poor math capabilities.

The most common math mistake is missing a zero in a calculation and being off by an order of magnitude. For example, if the correct answer to the calculation is 10M, candidates may miss a zero and arrive at 1M as the answer. The solution to this is to minimize the number of zeros in your numbers by using "K," "M," and "B" to represent one thousand, one million, and one billion respectively in your calculations.

You should know that:

- 1,000 = 1K

- 1,000,000 = 1M = 1,000K

- 1,000,000,000 = 1B = 1,000M = 1,000,000K

Example: We have sold eleven million cars at a price of seventeen thousand dollars. How much revenue is that?

$11M * $17K

($11 * $17) * (M * K)

($187) * (B)

$187B in revenue

Example: We have $143,000,000 in revenue and 13,000 customers. What is the average spend per customer?

$143M / 13K

($143 / 13) * (M / K)

($11) * (K)

$11K spend per customer

Another strategy for minimizing math mistakes is to do your calculation a second time quickly to see if you arrive at the same number. While this strategy works, the downside is that if you do this too many times or take too long to do your second calculation, the interviewer may interpret that as a sign of weakness in your math capabilities.

A third strategy is to do a quick sense check of your final answer before communicating it to the interviewer. This is something you should be doing every time you do a calculation and get an answer.

To do this, you can ask yourself the following questions:

- Does this number make sense and seem reasonable?
- Do I think this number is too low or too high?
- Is there another number that I can benchmark or compare this to?

You can differentiate yourself from other candidates by talking through your sense check out loud. This shows the interviewer that you are not just calculating numbers like a robot, but conceptualizing the number to understand what it means and if it makes sense.

Example: You perform a calculation and determine there are 3M cars in the US.

> "I am getting that there are 3M cars in the US. Let me do a quick sense check of this number. There are roughly 300M

people in the US, and if there are 3M cars, that means 1% of the population has a car. This does not make sense, because that figure is too low. Let me go back and see where I may have missed a zero."

Example: You perform a calculation and determine that a large telecommunication company has annual revenues of $100B.

"The revenue I have calculated is $100B. Let me do a quick sense check of this number. I interned at a large telecommunication company last summer and know that they have revenues of roughly $160B. The revenue I have just calculated is also for a large telecommunication company, and is roughly the same order of magnitude. Therefore, I think the $100B revenue figure is reasonable."

IX. Answering Qualitative Business Questions

Qualitative business questions test your logic, reasoning, and general business intuition for basic business concepts.

This is what the interviewer is looking for:

- Basic knowledge of business terms and principles

- Astute, sharp business intuition

- Structured responses to qualitative business questions

- Ability to communicate in a clear, concise, and confident way

In order to answer qualitative business questions, it is helpful to have some basic business knowledge so that you are familiar with basic terms and principles. This will help you develop an astute, sharp business intuition for case interviews. Business/economics majors and MBA candidates usually have acquired this knowledge through the classes that they have taken. However, if you are not a business/economics major or MBA candidate, don't worry because there is very little business knowledge that you need to know. You will also quickly learn and develop an astute, sharp business intuition from doing practice case interviews.

I have included a short business crash course reading below for the basics of what you need to know. Even if you have a strong business background, the following is worth a quick read or skim as these business terms and principles show up frequently in case interviews.

Fundamentals of business knowledge

Market Share: Market share is a way of measuring how much of a presence a company has in a particular market. Mathematically, it is calculated by taking the revenue a company has in a given market and dividing it by the size of the market. Therefore, market share is always between 0-100%.

Market Share = Revenue earned in a market ($) / Size of the market ($)

Say, for example, that a pet food manufacturer has revenues of $10B. If the size of the pet food market is $50B, then that pet food manufacturer has a 20% market share. ($10B/$50B)

A company with 80% market share has a significantly large presence in the market. Conversely, a company with <1% market share has a tiny presence in the market.

Profit margin: Profit margin measures how much a company takes in from selling a product once costs have been accounted for. It is calculated by taking the profit and dividing it by the price of the product or revenue.

Profit Margin = Profit ($) / Revenue ($)

If I am selling pizzas for $10, but it costs me roughly $6 to make a pizza, then my profit margin is 40% ($4 profit/$10 price).

Generally, companies want to invest more in higher margin products because they make more money off of them. Lower margin products are generally not as attractive because companies keep a smaller percentage of what these products sell for, and they are at risk of not being profitable if costs go up or if they have to lower price to compete with other competitors.

Return on investment (ROI): ROI is a metric used to determine how attractive a particular investment is. Mathematically, it is calculated by taking the profit from the investment and dividing it by the total investment cost for a given time period. There are 1-year ROI calculations, 3-year ROI calculations, 10-year ROI calculations, and so on. When calculating ROI make sure to clarify what the time horizon is for the calculation.

ROI = Profit from Investment ($) / Investment Cost ($)

Let's say, for example, that I can invest $50K in a friend's pet shop and expect a profit of $65K over the next two years. The alternative option is to invest $12K in a coworker's novel and earn $24K profit in the next two years. In these two examples, we are interested in the 2-year ROI.

The pet shop has an ROI of 1.3x ($65K/$50k) while the novel has an ROI of 2x ($24K/$12K). So, the novel is a much more attractive investment since I am getting higher returns for a given amount of investment. However, note that in absolute dollars, the pet shop would give you more money. The pet shop would net you $15K ($65K - $50K) while the novel would only net you $12K ($24K - $12K). However, the novel has the higher ROI.

Barriers to entry: Barriers to entry are simply the obstacles that a company would need to overcome to enter a new market. Examples of barriers to entry are: capital, technical knowledge/expertise, brand name, distribution channels, economies of scale, technology, government regulation, and product differentiation.

Variable and fixed costs: Costs can be categorized into either variable costs or fixed costs. The difference between the two is that variable costs increase directly with the number or quantity of product that is made while fixed costs do not. You can also think about it this way: if you were to produce one more unit of product, variable costs are the costs associated with producing that one extra unit.

Let's say that your business is selling pizza. The dough, the cheese, the tomato sauce, and the toppings would all be variable costs. If you were to produce one more pizza, you'd have to pay for more of these ingredients.

Fixed costs on the other hand, do not change directly as the number or quantity of product changes. In the pizza example, an example of fixed costs would be rent that you pay for the building. If you were to produce one extra pizza, you would still pay the same amount of rent. Other examples of fixed costs are: utilities (electricity, gas, etc.), salaries of workers (you would pay their salaries regardless of how many pizzas are produced), and equipment/machines.

Fragmented vs. concentrated market: Fragmented and concentrated are two different ways to describe the competitiveness of a market. They are on opposite ends of the market competitiveness spectrum.

A fragmented market is composed of many different companies, with no company having a significantly large market share. For example, a market with 100 different players each with 1% market share would be a highly fragmented market.

A concentrated market is the opposite. Concentrated markets usually have a few players that collectively have a large market share. For example, a market where the top four players have 90% of the market share would be a highly concentrated market.

The competitiveness of the market generally determines how high the barriers to entry are. For a fragmented market, there are generally low barriers to entry. The rationale behind this is that if there were high barriers to entry, there would not be so many players participating in the market. A concentrated market has high barriers to entry. The rationale behind that is that there are only a few large players in the market because they were the only ones capable of overcoming the high barriers to entry.

Generally, it is easier to enter a fragmented market since the barriers to entry are low. A concentrated market can only be entered if the high barriers to entry are met, making it much more difficult.

Supplier, manufacturer, distributor, and retailer: A supplier is typically referred to as the company that sells raw materials to another company, who then uses the raw materials to create a product to sell in the market. The company that uses the raw materials to create the final product is known as the manufacturer. A distributor is typically a company that transports the final product to places where the product can be sold. Retailers are companies that sell the product.

Some companies do all four of these things: they gather their own raw materials, manufacture their own product, distribute their product to their stores, and sell their product through their own stores. Other companies may only do one of these things.

For example, let's say that your company makes frozen pizzas that are sold in local grocery stores and large supermarkets. The supplier would be the companies that you buy the dough, tomato sauce, cheese, and toppings from. Your company then converts these raw materials into the final product, a frozen pizza, making your company the manufacturer. The distributor could be the trucking company that takes the final product that is frozen pizza, and delivers them to grocery stores and supermarkets, which are the retailers.

Pricing strategy: There are many different ways to price a product or an offering. Which method is best depends on the situation and on what information is available. Each method has their own advantages and disadvantages.

The first way to price a product is to determine how much a customer is willing to pay for the product. This is usually done through customer surveys and focus groups and is the most straight forward approach. However, sometimes customers do not know how much they'd pay for a hypothetical product, which is one thing to consider when using this method.

A second way to price a product is to look at what price competitors are selling their products for. You can then price your product within the competitors' range. The disadvantage of this method is that it only works if competitors offer the same or similar product to what you are trying to sell.

A third way to price a product is to look at how much it costs to produce the product. You can then assign a profit margin to that product and set the price accordingly. This method guarantees that the product will have a certain profit margin when sold, but does not consider the customer's willingness to buy the product at that given price point.

Buyer power (or purchasing power): Buyer power is a qualitative measure of how much power a company has in setting the price of raw materials or services that it purchases from a supplier.

For example, let's say that there are two wooden furniture manufacturers that each have 50% market share and purchase wood, the raw material, from suppliers. Let's say that there are hundreds of different suppliers of wood. In this scenario, the wooden furniture manufacturers have very strong or high buying power. There are only two players that purchase wood, but hundreds of different players that sell wood. Because of this discrepancy, the wood sellers are more likely to sell wood at a discounted price because there are only two players who they can sell to, and they are competing with the other hundreds of sellers. For the wooden furniture manufacturers, it is very likely that they will be able to purchase wood at a preferred lower price point.

In the reverse scenario, let's say that there are hundreds of cherry pie producers that each have <1% market share. Let's assume that there are only two cherry suppliers in the market that sell raw cherries. In this scenario, the cherry pie producers have very low buying power. Since there are only two suppliers of cherries, but hundreds of cherry pie producers that need to purchase these cherries, suppliers do not need to offer discounts or reduced prices in order to be able to sell their raw materials. It is unlikely that the cherry pie producers will be able to purchase cherries at a price point that they are happy with since they have low buying power.

In summary, buyer power is high or strong if buyers are more concentrated than sellers. However, buyer power can also be strong if there are many substitutes for the raw material that they are buying, and if the costs of switching to a substitute raw material is low.

For example, let's say that a beef hot dog player purchases beef to make hot dogs. If suddenly pork prices drop to a historic low, and it is relatively easy for the hot dog player to switch to producing pork hot dogs, then that player may have strong buyer power even if the beef hot dog producer market is not heavily concentrated. The beef hot dog player can ask for a lower price point from suppliers, and threaten to switch to pork if prices are not met.

Reasons for making a merger/acquisition: There are many different reasons why a company would want to buy or merge with another company. The most common reason tends to be that a company is lacking a particular product or offering in their portfolio. Rather than invest the resources organically to develop that product or offering, the company instead decides to acquire another company that has that product or offering. This is done because it might be easier and/or cheaper to acquire that missing product into the portfolio rather than developing it themselves from scratch.

A second common reason is for synergies. A synergy occurs when the interaction of two parts (in this example, two companies) produces a combined positive effect or outcome that is greater than the sum of the two individual parts.

For example, if Company A, worth $7B, and Company B, worth $3B, merge and have revenue synergies, then the combined value of Company A and Company B could be $11B. This is $1B more than the sum of the two parts had they been separate companies.

Synergies can be broken down into revenue synergies and cost synergies. Examples of revenue synergies include: having access to a new customer base or market, being able to cross-sell products to existing customers, and sharing overlapping infrastructure or distribution channels. Examples of cost synergies include: headcount reduction from eliminating redundancies, reduced overhead or fixed costs from consolidating functions (e.g. HR, marketing), and increased buying power.

The third reason why a company would acquire another company is because they see a smaller, high-growth competitor as a threat. By acquiring the company, this eliminates such a threat. Doing acquisitions is a way to grow the company and increase market share without doing much work.

The fourth reason is that a company may purchase another company just to diversify its portfolio.

For example, a beer company might purchase a soda company. Had the beer company not purchased the soda company and a lot of people stopped drinking beer, then the company would see a huge drop in revenue. However, if the company had acquired a soda company, the drop in revenue would not be as large because they also sell soda, and soda sales may not have necessarily dropped if beer consumption drops.

Private equity: The short, simplified definition of private equity is that private equity is comprised of firms that generally have a lot of money, that invest and/or purchase other companies for the sake of getting a return on investment (ROI) in one way or another.

One way that they can get an ROI is by purchasing companies that are not performing well that may or may not be profitable. They then turn these companies around so that they are performing well and profitable. Private equity firms would then sell off these companies at a higher price than what these companies were originally purchased for. You can think of this strategy as "flipping companies," much like a stock trader would flip stocks.

For mergers and acquisitions, companies that are not doing well and are not profitable are generally not attractive targets to acquire. However, for private equity firms, this is not the case because they sometimes target these underperforming companies, turn them around, and then sell for profit.

A second way that private equity firms can get an ROI is by purchasing a company that would create synergies with the rest of their portfolio. Remember, private equity firms can own many different companies at the same time in their portfolio. The synergies from an investment or purchase could enhance or increase their overall portfolio ROI in the long-run.

If you get a case involving private equity, make sure to ask for what strategy the private equity firm is looking to use to get an ROI. This will dictate what qualities you need to look for in the companies that may get bought out by the private equity firm.

Price sensitivity: Price sensitivity measures the change in quantity of a product that a customer will purchase if the price changes. If a customer is highly price sensitive, even a small increase in price may cause them to stop buying the product altogether. If a customer is not price sensitive at all, a small increase in price will not cause them to purchase any less product.

For example, suppose you are price sensitive to clothes. If a particular brand that you like has increased the prices of their clothing, you are likely to purchase less from them. This is because there are many other brands of clothing that you could purchase from, and because you most likely don't have an immediate need to purchase new clothes.

In a different scenario, if you are diabetic, you are probably not price sensitive to insulin shots. Why? First of all, there are no substitutes for insulin shots because that is the only way for diabetics to keep their blood sugar levels under control. Secondly, diabetics must buy insulin shots because if they don't, they could die. Therefore, if the price of insulin shots increases, customers will continue buying regardless.

In summary, just remember that increasing the price of a product may not necessarily increase revenues due to price sensitivity. It is important to figure out if the incremental revenue that you get from increasing the price is greater than the loss of revenue from selling less product. The same logic applies for when you are decreasing the price of a product.

Ways to increase revenues: Revenue can be increased organically and inorganically. Organic revenue growth is revenue growth that a company achieves through its own efforts, internal to the company. Inorganic growth is growth through a merger or acquisition, done externally.

Let's look into organic growth first. First, revenue can be increased by increasing revenue from existing products. This can be done by either increasing the quantity sold of the product or by changing the price (remember which direction to change the price depends on price sensitivity of the customers). Secondly, revenue can be increased by selling entirely new products that you did not previously offer.

For inorganic growth, merging or acquiring a company increases revenue because you naturally will take in the revenue of the acquired company.

Ways to decrease costs: We can think of reducing costs by either reducing variable costs or reducing fixed costs.

Fixed costs are generally more difficult to reduce because fixed costs are determined in the longer-run and have contracts or "locked-in" costs that last for many years. For example, once equipment purchases are made, they generally can't have their costs reduced since they are already purchased and are being used for many years to come. However, fixed costs could be potentially reduced if contracts are renegotiated, but the likelihood of this is lower than the chance of reducing variable costs.

For example, the costs of rent for a warehouse (a fixed cost) could be decreased if renegotiated with the landlord.

Variable costs tend to be easier to reduce. One way is that the company can switch to a supplier that sells the same raw material at a cheaper price. If the same raw material cannot be bought at a cheaper price, the company can look for substitutes for that raw material, but this is not always possible. Another way is that the company can try to use less of each raw material in the production process. However, note that any of these changes could affect the quality of the product. As with fixed costs, another way to reduce costs would be to renegotiate prices of raw materials with the current supplier.

For example, a US toy manufacturer switches their plastic supplier to a vendor in China in order to reduce the costs of plastic, a variable cost.

Economies of scale: Economies of scale is the advantage that a company gets in terms of buying power as it produces and sells more and more product. As companies grow, they generally sell more and more product such that they have more buying power from suppliers. The increased buying power allows the company to purchase raw materials and other variable costs at much lower prices than competitors. This allows the company to price their product at a lower price point. The lower price, in turn, allows them to sell even more product, which results in even more increased buying power. This cycle can repeat as the company continues to grow.

The cycle described above is referred to as the process of a company achieving economies of scale. The company's costs get lower and lower while they sell more and more product. This cycle eventually does stop when suppliers are no longer able to reduce the costs of raw materials that they can sell, because they too need to make a profit off of the sale of raw materials. At this point, the company has achieved the maximum benefit of economies of scale.

Companies that have achieved economies of scale are buying raw materials at the lowest price point possible, allowing them to sell a large quantity of product and achieve high market share.

How to answer qualitative business questions

The following are some examples of qualitative business questions that you may get asked. Unfortunately, it is not possible for me to list every possible qualitative question that you will get. There are way too many possible questions. I just want to give you a sense of the type of questions that you may be asked and the level of detail you are expected to answer them at. Note that none of these questions require very specific business jargon or technical knowledge.

- What are some barriers to entry in the cable TV market?

- What are some variable and fixed costs that you can think of for starting a food truck?

- What are some reasons for why a pharmaceutical company would buy another pharmaceutical company?

- What are some ways to increase video game revenue?

- How can we decrease manufacturing costs of wooden furniture?

- How much market share do you think we can capture in this new market?

- Looking at our portfolio of four products. Which ones should we invest heavily in? Which ones should we divest?

- What are some ways we can price this new product?

- Do you think this is a competitive market?

So how do you differentiate yourself from the thousands of other candidates out there? There are several ways that you can do this.

First of all, structure. I would say that when asked a qualitative business question, most candidates will immediately start talking off the top of their heads about any ideas or thoughts that they have. To differentiate yourself, I recommend that you take an extra five to ten seconds to structure your answer. What do I mean by this?

For example, let's take a look at two different responses to a qualitative question such as: "What are some benefits to hosting the Super Bowl?"

An ordinary candidate might say something like this:

> "There are many benefits to hosting the Super Bowl. First of all, you can bring money into the city from selling tickets to the event. Secondly, you can bring national attention and recognition to the city, since the entire US will likely be watching it on television or keeping up with it. Third, an increase in guests will probably lead to increased spending in the city economy overall."

While this answer definitely works and makes sense, one critique is that the candidate simply listed the top three random ideas that came to their head. For this reason, the response may appear to ramble on or repeat a few points.

Compare this answer to the following one from a candidate who spent an extra five to ten seconds structuring their response:

> "There are both short-term and long-term benefits that can be realized from hosting the Super Bowl. Starting with the short-term benefits, the big thing that comes to mind is revenue. Hosting the Super Bowl can bring revenue into the city, from ticket sales to hotel and housing spend, food and drink consumption, and general tourist purchases. For the long-term benefits, one such benefit would be city branding/reputation. With the entire US keeping up with the Super Bowl, this is a long-term opportunity for the city to create a positive image of itself to encourage future tourism."

Notice how much more organized and easy to follow this second answer is from the first? Having a simple structure to your qualitative answers makes a big difference in differentiating yourself from the other candidates.

Here is a list of quick mini-frameworks that you can leverage to structure your answer:

- Internal/external
- Short-term/long-term
- Economic/non-economic
- Quantitative/qualitative

By using these pairings of words, your answers will be much more organized than the majority of the rest of the candidates.

The second way to differentiate yourself is from creative brainstorming. You can show creativity in two different ways.

The first way is to simply list a large quantity of ideas. For example, if a candidate is asked for barriers to entry in a particular market and is only able to come up with two ideas, that candidate has probably given an answer that is very average among candidates. However, if one candidate comes in and is able to list seven or eight ideas (this is quite a lot; I am exaggerating the number to illustrate this example), then that candidate has differentiated themselves from the pack.

The second way to demonstrate creativity is to come up with an idea that none of the other candidates had thought of. Some people can naturally come up with more creative and unique ideas than others. However, it is very difficult to improve on this skill in a short period of time.

With that said, I recommend that you invest the majority of your time on structuring your responses and being able to come up with many ideas for each qualitative question. This will differentiate yourself from the rest of the candidates.

X. Delivering a Conclusion

Delivering the conclusion is the last impression that you will leave with the interviewer. Therefore, it is important that you deliver a solid conclusion and recommendation.

A good conclusion and recommendation satisfies the following criteria:

1. Starts with a confident, assertive recommendation

2. Is structured

3. Includes next steps

During this part of the case, the interviewer is looking for your:

- Ability to synthesize all of the information discussed during the case and pull out the key takeaways

- Ability to deliver a firm recommendation backed by facts, business acumen, and judgement

- Ability to communicate in a clear, concise, and confident way

For the first criteria, make sure that your conclusion starts with your recommendation. The very first sentence of your conclusion should state an assertive recommendation.

One common mistake many candidates make is that they begin their conclusion by summarizing the problem, and then describing the process and the steps that they have gone through before arriving at the recommendation. For case interviews, you want to start with the recommendation first. The answer should come first, not last.

The second common mistake is that when prompted for a recommendation, candidates will often heavily hedge their recommendation. However, interviewers might interpret this as you being unconfident and unassertive. Even if you feel that your recommendation might not be the correct one, I recommend that you pick a side and present your recommendation in a firm and assertive manner. If you feel strongly that your recommendation may not be correct, you can hedge your recommendation in the "next steps" portion of the conclusion.

For the second criteria, structure is highly important for the conclusion. I would recommend that you use a structure similar to the one below. It is simple, clean, and effective.

A structured conclusion should look something like this:

- I recommend that we (insert recommendation) for the following three reasons:
    - 1) ...
    - 2) ...
    - 3) ...

- For these reasons, I recommend that we (insert recommendation)

- For next steps, I would like to look into the following two things:
    - 1) ...
    - 2) ...

For the third criteria, including "next steps" in your conclusion is important because it shows that you are thinking ahead of areas that you would like to further look into if you had more time. Most candidates do not discuss next steps, so including this part can help you differentiate yourself from the other candidates.

You shouldn't necessarily be doing any novel thinking to come up with next steps. During the case interview, there should have naturally been a couple of points where you wished you had more information or where you wanted to do another piece of analysis.

You can use these points as your next steps. Therefore, next steps should not always be new ideas that the interviewer is hearing for the first time.

For example, leveraging the structure above, a strong recommendation and conclusion would sound something like this:

> "I recommend that we do not enter the peanut butter market for the following three reasons.
>
> One, we looked at the competitive landscape and learned that the top four players have 90% of the market share. This suggests that the market is highly concentrated with high barriers to entry.
>
> Two, we looked into possible synergies with our existing strawberry jam product. Peanut butter and strawberry jam have little to no synergies. We would have to buy new equipment and develop a proprietary peanut butter recipe to enter the peanut butter market.
>
> Three, we looked at the financial considerations and determined it would take ten years for us to break even in this market. Since management is looking for additional profit in the next two to three years, entering the market does not make sense financially.
>
> For these reasons, I recommend that we do not enter the peanut butter market.
>
> For next steps, I would like to look into the following two things to further confirm my recommendation. One, I'd like to look into the overlap between strawberry jam customers and peanut butter customers. If there is no overlap, we probably can't cross-sell strawberry jam with peanut butter and leverage our existing customer relationships. Two, since it doesn't seem like we want to enter the market organically, it may be worth looking into partnerships or strategic alliances to see if these are attractive enough for us to consider entering the market inorganically."

Transitioning from solving the case to presenting a recommendation and conclusion can be fairly challenging. During the case, you most likely will have covered quite a bit of ground on a variety of topics. The challenging part of the conclusion is pulling together all of the key findings that you have discovered and determining what these key findings mean for the answer.

You should have been taking brief notes on key takeaways throughout the case on your note sheet. Having done this, you simply need to quickly scan through your notes to review what the key takeaways are, and think about what that means for the answer.

It is acceptable for candidates to ask their interviewer for 30 seconds to read through their notes and organize their thoughts before delivering a structured conclusion. However, if your interviewer gives you time to think through the conclusion, they will expect more structure from you than if you immediately started delivering your recommendation and conclusion when prompted for a summary. Make sure your conclusion is structured if you are going to be asking for time to gather your thoughts.

XI. Everything You Need to Memorize

There are not that many things you need to memorize for case interviews. More of it comes down to understanding and mastering concepts. This comes with practice. Below are all of the things that we've covered that should be memorized.

Eight Buckets for Developing a Structured Framework

1. Market attractiveness

2. Competitive landscape

3. Company attractiveness OR company capabilities

4. Customer segmentation and needs

5. Financial considerations

6. Risks and mitigations

7. Synergies

8. Create your own bucket

Mini-Frameworks to Structure Answers to Qualitative Questions

- Internal/external

- Short-term/long-term

- Economic/non-economic

- Quantitative/qualitative

Market Sizing Statistics to Know

- U.S. population is 300M or 320M (use whichever number is easier to do math with)

- World population is 7B

Math Equations

- The Profit Equation
    - *Profit = (Quantity * Price) − [(Quantity * Variable Costs) + Fixed Costs]*

- The Breakeven Equation
    - *Quantity * (Price − Variable Costs) = Fixed Costs*

Structure for Conclusion

- I recommend that we (insert recommendation) for the following three reasons:
    - 1) …
    - 2) …
    - 3) …

- For these reasons, I recommend that we (insert recommendation)

- For next steps, I would like to look into the following two things:
    - 1) …
    - 2) …

If you found this book helpful and want even more detailed explanations, examples, practice problems, real practice cases, and strategies, I've created a one-week case interview online crash course that can be found at **HackingTheCaseInterview.com**

The goal of the crash course is to help you pass your upcoming interview in the shortest amount of time possible. It is an all-inclusive course that contains (1) all of the strategies and knowledge you need to know, and (2) all of the practice problems and practice cases you need to do to be competent.

Overview of the One-Week Case Interview Crash Course

- Engage with 50+ concise video lessons that consolidate hundreds of hours of knowledge and experience

- Hone your case interview skills through 20 real, full-length practice cases, with detailed solutions and feedback

- Learn an advanced framework strategy to tackle non-traditional case problems typically given in final round interviews

- Review and practice understanding and interpreting the 10 types of charts and graphs you'll see in a case interview

- Practice and refine your newly learned strategies with quality practice problems in every section

If you found this book helpful, I highly recommend checking out **HackingTheCaseInterview.com** to take what you've learned in this book to the next level.

Introduction to Doing Practice Cases

Where to find practice cases

There are five practice cases in this book. Once you finish these, there are hundreds, if not thousands, of cases out there on the internet, most available for free. You can do a quick internet search for "consulting business school casebooks." If your school has a consulting club, they will likely have many casebooks as well. Be aware that these cases may be hit or miss in terms of quality. **HackingTheCaseInterview.com** has 20 real, high-quality practice cases with detailed solutions.

How to do practice cases effectively

The best way to do practice cases is to simulate a real case interview as closely as you can. That means putting away all books and notes, not using a calculator, and not taking breaks during a practice case.

I strongly recommend that you do all practice cases with a case interview partner, who will deliver the case to you and provide feedback. You can find case interview partners at your school. There are also resources online where you can find others around the world to practice cases through video or phone call.

Choose your case interview partner carefully, as they will make all the difference on how quickly you will get better. Ideally, you want to pick someone who is:

- Experienced with case interviews
- Capable of delivering detailed, tactical, and actionable feedback
- Determined and motivated to practice many cases
- Available to practice cases when you have the time

If your case interview partner doesn't deliver cases the right way or provides mediocre feedback, they will not be helpful to you.

How it typically works with a case interview partner is that one of you will be the interviewer and the other the candidate. The interviewer will read the entire practice case interview beforehand to know exactly how the case will proceed and what information is available to give the candidate. The interviewer will then deliver the case to the candidate. A practice case should take 45 minutes to an hour to complete. At the end of the case, the interviewer will give feedback to the candidate. The feedback session should take about 15 minutes, possibly even 30 minutes if you are new to doing cases.

For the next case, roles will be switched. The interviewer will be the candidate, and the candidate will be the interviewer.

By the time you complete ten practice cases, you will also have given ten practice cases. You may feel that you are wasting your time giving someone else a practice case, but you can learn quite a bit by giving practice cases. You can understand how someone else approaches solving a case and can leverage that in the future. You also put yourself in the shoes of an interviewer and attain a better understanding of what interviewers are looking for.

It may be helpful to video record yourself during practice case interviews. This way you can analyze your body gestures and speaking patterns. Oftentimes, you'll be surprised with your body language or what you say during a practice case. I wouldn't do this with every practice case, but I'd try to do this every time you feel that you have taken a significant step forward.

Practice cases in this book

Although I strongly encourage you to practice case interviews with a partner, the practice cases in this book are written so that you can do them alone or with a partner. However, after these first few cases, you should definitely be doing case interviews live with a case interview partner.

Practice Case #1 – It's Wine O'Clock Somewhere

Difficulty: Beginner

The company you are working with is called Beer Co. They manufacture, distribute, and sell over a hundred different varieties of beer, including lagers, pilsners, ales, and stouts in the US. They sell to restaurants, bars, wholesale retailers, and directly to consumers. Recently, however, they have been experiencing a decline in revenue across the majority of their beer products.

Because of this, the VP of Business Strategy has considered entering the wine market in hopes of increasing revenue and profit.

Should Beer Co. enter the wine market?

(Sample framework is on the following page)

<u>Sample Framework</u>: One possible framework could look something like the following. The candidate does not need to have this exact framework, but should capture most of these points.

- Attractiveness of the wine market
    - What is the size of the wine market?
    - What is the growth rate of the wine market?
    - What are the average profit margins for a wine producer in this market?
    - How do these compare to the beer market?

- Competitive landscape of the wine market
    - How many competitors are in the market?
    - How much share does each player have?
    - What are the barriers to entry for this market?

- Beer Co.'s capabilities to enter the wine market
    - What existing capabilities can Beer Co. leverage to enter the wine market?
    - Does Beer Co. have sufficient capital to enter the market?

- Financial considerations
    - Will it be profitable to manufacture and sell wine?
    - How long will it take to break even if Beer Co. enters the wine market?

Question 1: Let's begin by determining the market size of wine in the US. Is the wine market a large market?

(Sample answer is on the following page)

Answer to Question 1: Remember, the final answer that the candidate comes up with does not matter. What matters is the approach that the candidate takes and the proficiency at which they do math.

Structure for determining the market size for wine in the US:

- Start with the US population

- Segment the US population by age

- Estimate what percentage of each age group consumes wine

- Estimate how many bottles of wine a wine drinker consumes in a year

- Estimate the average price of a bottle of wine

- Multiply across these numbers to determine the market size of wine

Let's assume that the US population is 320M people. Let's divide the US population into four different segments: (0-20), (20-40), (40-60), and (60-80). Each segment has 80M people.

For (0-20), let's assume 0% of people drink wine because consuming alcohol under the age of 21 is illegal in the US. Therefore, 0M wine drinkers in this segment. (0% * 80M)

For (20-40), let's assume 30% of people drink wine based on our personal experiences with friends and family members' drinking preferences. Therefore, there are 24M wine drinkers in this segment. (30% * 80M)

For (40-60), let's assume 30% of people drink wine as well based on personal experiences. Therefore, there are 24M wine drinkers in this segment. (30% * 80M)

For (60-80), let's assume that 15% of people drink wine. The rationale behind this is that as people reach this older age segment, they must be more careful of what they eat and drink due to health concerns. Therefore, there are 12M wine drinkers in this segment. (15% * 80M)

Adding up the wine drinkers across these four age segments, we get 60M wine drinkers. (24M + 24M + 12M)

Next, let's assume that wine drinkers consume one bottle every week. There are 52 weeks a year, but let's assume 50 weeks to make the calculations simpler. Therefore, each wine drinker consumes 50 bottles of wine in a year.

From this, we calculate that there are 3B bottles of wine consumed a year in the US (60M * 50)

Based on personal experiences, let's say that the average bottle of wine is $20. Therefore, the market size of wine in the US is **$60B**. (3B * $20)

To determine if we consider the wine market to be large, we need to compare the market size to something else. In this case interview, it makes sense to compare it to the size of the beer market.

If the candidate asks, the size of the beer market is **$40B**. Therefore, the candidate should use this benchmark to compare with the size of the wine market in order to rationalize whether or not the wine market is a large market.

Question 2: Let's say that the top three players in the wine market have 80% of the market share. What does this tell you about the barriers to entry? What are some examples of barriers to entry in this market?

(Sample answer is on the following page)

<u>Answer to Question 2</u>: The fact that the top three players have 80% of the market share means that the market is very concentrated. Since there are only a few major players in the market, barriers to entry into the wine market are likely high.

Barriers to entry can be segmented into two buckets: economic barriers to entry and non-economic barriers to entry.

- Economic barriers to entry
    - Capital required to purchase the equipment for wine production
    - Fertile, suitable land to grow grapes
    - Distribution channels and infrastructure to reach and deliver to customers
    - Economies of scale to have cost advantages

- Non-economic barriers to entry
    - Brand name in the wine market
    - Knowledge/expertise to produce superior wine
    - Product differentiation for the wine being produced
    - Time required for wine to age

Question 3: Next, let's take a look at Beer Co.'s current capabilities. Do you think there are any synergies that can be realized between producing beer and producing wine?

(Sample answer is on the following page)

Answer to Question 3: It does not matter whether the candidate says that there are few synergies or many synergies. The important thing to look for is whether the answer is structured and logical. A sample answer is shown below.

There does not appear to be many synergies between beer and wine. Let's think about three different types of synergies: synergies arising from manufacturing of product, synergies arising from shared customers, and synergies arising from the workforce.

Synergies arising from manufacturing of product: There are not many synergies arising from the production of both wine and beer. Wine comes from grapes, while beer comes from barley, corn, or rice. Therefore, they do not share much raw materials. On top of that, the process in which wine and beer ferments is likely different, so the same machines and storage probably can't be used.

Synergies arising from shared customers: There could be some customer sharing between wine drinkers and beer drinkers. However, I'd imagine that the overlap is not that large. People who like beer will buy predominantly beer, while people that like wine will predominantly buy wine.

Synergies arising from the workforce: There are not a whole lot of synergies here because the skills needed to produce beer and wine are different. Beer and wine come from different raw materials, and the process to produce the two products are very different. Therefore, employees who produce beer may not be able to help with producing wine without substantial training. The same could be said about employees who produce wine.

Conclusion: Let's say that the VP of Business Strategy has just walked in and wants a preliminary summary and recommendation of what you have learned so far. What do you say?

(Sample conclusion is on the following page)

<u>Sample Conclusion</u>: It does not matter whether the recommendation is to enter the market or not to enter the market. As long as the conclusion is structured and is backed up by the points previously discussed, the conclusion will work.

I recommend that we do not enter the wine market for the following three reasons:

One, the wine market has high barriers to entry. The market is concentrated with the top three players having 80% of the market share. It will be difficult to enter this market because of a variety of barriers, such as capital, the knowledge/expertise to produce superior wine, and brand name.

Two, although the market size is relatively large at $60M, compared to $40M that is the beer market, we will not be likely to capture much market share because of the high barriers to entry.

Three, there are very little synergies between producing beer and wine. The two products have different raw ingredients, and the production process is quite different.

Therefore, I recommend that we do not enter the wine market.

However, given more time, there are two things that I'd like to look into to further validate my recommendation. One, I'd like to look into existing capabilities that Beer Co. can leverage to enter the market. Two, I'd like to do a breakeven analysis to determine if entering the wine market will even be profitable.

Author Commentary: Market entry and profitability cases are the two most common cases for first-round interviews. This case is a very standard market entry case. Expect to be given a market sizing problem or profit/breakeven calculation, followed by a few qualitative questions in a first-round interview.

You should practice to be able to develop a framework for any market entry case quickly and easily. Because it is so common, this is an essential framework to have in your back pocket.

Practice Case #2 – Clothes Woes

Difficulty: Beginner

The client who has hired you is a clothing manufacturer. They make daily-wear clothing for both men and women. They sell their clothing at their own physical stores in malls around the world. The clothing company was doing quite well and were very profitable a few years ago. However, profits have gone down significantly since then.

What is causing the decline in profits? What can be done to address and fix this problem?

(Sample framework is on the following page)

<u>Sample Framework</u>: One possible framework could look something like the following. The candidate does not need to have this exact framework, but should capture most of these points.

- Financial situation
    - How has revenue changed during this time period?
        - Quantity
        - Price
    - How have costs changed during this time period?
        - Fixed Costs
        - Variable Costs

- Customer segments
    - Have customer preferences changed during this time period?
    - Do customers perceive or view our company differently than before?

- Competitive landscape of the clothing market
    - Have new competitors entered the market?
    - Are competitors doing something different than what they were doing previously?

- Clothing market
    - Has profitability declined for the clothing market overall?
    - Are there new government regulations affecting clothing manufacturing?
    - Are there new technologies disrupting the clothing market?

Question 1: Let's begin by looking at revenues and profit margins of the different clothing product lines that we sell. How much have absolute profits decreased overall? Which product lines are seeing a decline in absolute profits?

Product	Before		
	Quantity Sold	Price Sold At	Profit Margin
Jackets	0.5M	$100	10%
Shirts	5M	$10	50%
Pants	3M	$30	30%
Shoes	1M	$50	20%

Product	Now		
	Quantity Sold	Price Sold At	Profit Margin
Jackets	1M	$100	5%
Shirts	4M	$10	40%
Pants	2.5M	$30	40%
Shoes	0.2M	$100	20%

(Sample answer is on the following page)

Answer to Question 1: To determine which product lines are seeing a decline in profits, we need to calculate profits for each product line for both before and now. From this we can see what product lines have a decline in profits.

Profits can be calculated by multiplying revenue by the profit margin. Revenue is calculated by multiplying the quantity sold and the price sold at. It is useful to create a summary table like the one below.

	Profit Before	Profit Now
Jackets	$5M	$5M
Shirts	$25M	$16M
Pants	$27M	$30M
Shoes	$10M	$4M
Total	$67M	$55M

Profits have decreased by **$12M** from $67M to $55M. The two product lines that are seeing a decline in absolute profits are **shirts (declined by $9M)** and **shoes (declined by $6M)**. The profits coming from jackets have not changed. The profits coming from pants have increased from $27M to $30M.

Question 2: Looking at the information that you have for quantity sold, price sold at, and profit margin for each of the product lines, what is causing each product's profits to change the way that it does? In other words, what explanation can you give for why each product's profits are changing?

(Sample answer is on the following page)

Answer to Question 2: Let's go through the different product lines one at a time.

Looking at jackets, the price has not changed between before and now. The reason why jackets have the same profits is because the quantity sold has doubled while the profit margin has halved. Therefore, profits have not changed.

Looking at shirts, the price has also not changed. The reason why shirts have decreased in revenue is because the quantity sold has decreased and the profit margin has decreased. Since price has not changed and margins have decreased, this implies that costs have increased. So, a decrease in quantity sold and an increase in costs is what is causing the decline in profits.

Looking at pants, the price has also not changed. Although the quantity sold has decreased, the profit margin for pants has increased enough such that profits overall for pants have increased.

Finally, looking at shoes, the profit margin has remained the same, but the price has increased significantly. It is possible that the increase in price has caused a drastic decrease in quantity sold due to customer price sensitivity. This is what has caused the decline in profits.

Question 3: Let's focus on shirts right now. Can you brainstorm different ways that we can increase profits for shirts?

(Sample answer is on the following page)

Answer to Question 3: Looking at shirts, we determined that the decrease in profits was due to both a decline in quantity sold and a decline in profit margin (meaning an increase in costs since price has stayed the same). Therefore, we can brainstorm different ways to increase profits both on the revenue side and cost side.

- Increase Revenue
    - Increase quantity sold
        - Marketing campaign to increase sales (TV ads, newspaper ads, radio broadcasting, flyers, celebrity endorsements, etc.)
        - Sell the shirt in more retail stores in different geographic regions
        - Sell shirts in bundles to encourage purchases of higher quantities
    - Change price
        - Increase price to increase revenue IF the quantity of shirts sold will not decrease significantly due to the increase in price
        - Decrease price to increase revenue IF the quantity of shirts sold will increase significantly due to the decrease in price

- Decrease Costs
    - Decrease variable costs
        - Renegotiate purchasing price for raw materials used to make the shirt
        - Use cheaper substitutes for raw materials used to make the shirt
        - Use less fabric to make each shirt (making the shirt thinner)
    - Decrease fixed costs
        - Invest in new equipment or technology that is more cost efficient to produce shirts
        - Renegotiate distributor or retailer contracts
        - Renegotiate salaries

Question 4: Now let's look at shoes. A popular, high-end department store has approached you to enter into a strategic partnership. Under the terms of the contract, you will not be able to sell shoes anymore. However, the department store will sell your shoes for you under their famous brand name. They will sell the shoe at $100 and promise that at least 1.2M shoes will be sold. The profit margins will still be 20%, but they will take 65% of the profits. You keep the rest of the profits.

Based purely on the economics of this deal, should you do this strategic partnership? Assume that without the partnership, shoe profits will be $4M, as they are now.

(Sample answer is on the following page)

Answer to Question 4: To determine whether to do this strategic partnership, we will compare profits that we would get from selling shoes ourselves with the expected profits we would get if we entered into this partnership.

If we do not enter the partnership, we will have shoe profits of $4M.

With the partnership, we will sell at least 1.2M shoes at $100. This means revenues will be at least $120M. Since profit margins are 20%, profits will be at least $24M. However, the high-end department store will take 65% of the profits. This means that we will collect 35% of the profits.

Therefore, your shoe profits will be **at least $8.4M**.

Based purely on economics, we should do this strategic partnership. We will increase shoe profits from $4M to at least $8.4M, more than doubling shoe profits.

Conclusion: Let's say that the CEO has just walked in and wants to know what is causing the decline in profits and what can be done to resolve these issues and increase profits? What do you say?

(Sample conclusion is on the following page)

Sample Conclusion: To increase profits, I recommend that we increase profits for the following two product lines: shirts and shoes. These are the two product lines that are causing the decline in profits for the company overall.

First, looking at shirts, profits have gone down because quantity sold has decreased and costs have increased, which drives a lower profit margin. To address this, we can look at both the revenue side and cost side.

On the revenue side, we can increase quantity sold by launching a marketing campaign, selling the shirt in more geographic regions, or bundling shirts together. We can also increase revenue by adjusting the price of the shirt.

On the cost side, we can try to reduce variable costs by renegotiating prices for raw materials or using cheaper substitutes for our raw materials. We can also try to reduce fixed costs by investing in more efficient equipment or renegotiating salary or retailer contracts.

Second, looking at shoes, we can increase profits by entering into a strategic partnership with a high-end department store. Although the department store will take 65% of profits, we will still expect profits to increase from $4M to at least $8.4M, more than doubling.

By addressing the decline in profits from shirts and shoes, we can increase profits for the company overall.

For next steps, I'd like to look into two things. One, I'd like to look into jackets to see if we can increase profits since profits for jackets have remained flat. Second, I'd like to look into pants and see if we can further increase profits because pants are the only product line that has increased in profits.

<u>Author Commentary</u>: Profitability and market sizing cases are the two most common cases for first-round interviews. This is a typical profitability case in which you dive into various revenue segments and determine what is at the root-cause of the profitability problem.

You should be able to work with numbers and calculations involving: quantity, price, revenue, costs, profit, and profit margin comfortably, without making any mathematical mistakes. This is another essential skill to have, especially for first-round interviews.

Practice Case #3 – Let's Bank on It

Difficulty: Moderate

Bank Co. is a large Nigerian bank that offers checking accounts and savings accounts to customers. They are the fourth largest bank in Nigeria and have over $10B in total deposits. Currently, Bank Co. does not offer credit cards to their customers while the top three banks do.

Bank Co. has done some diligences and has identified a possible credit card company acquisition target named Nigeria Card. Should Bank Co. acquire Nigeria Card so that they can offer credit cards to customers?

(Sample framework is on the following page)

<u>Sample Framework</u>: One possible framework could look something like the following. The candidate does not need to have this exact framework, but should capture most of these points.

- Financial considerations
    - Is Nigeria Card being acquired at a fair price?
    - How long will it take to break even from the acquisition costs?

- Nigeria Card company attractiveness
    - Is Nigeria Card profitable?
    - How much market share does Nigeria Card have?
    - How is the brand name of Nigeria Card perceived by customers?
    - Does Nigeria Card have any capabilities or offerings that differentiates itself from competitors?

- Credit Card market attractiveness
    - What is the size of the credit card market?
    - What is the growth rate of the credit card market?
    - What are the profit margins like in the credit card market?

- Synergies
    - Are there any revenue synergies between banking accounts and credit cards?
    - Are there any cost synergies?

Question 1: Before we look into the financial considerations, let's think about synergies between a banking company and a credit card company. Are there any synergies that can be realized from this acquisition?

(Sample answer is on the following page)

<u>Answer to Question 1</u>: It does not matter whether the candidate says that there are few synergies or many synergies. The important thing to look for is whether the answer is structured and logical. A sample answer is shown below.

There are several synergies that can be realized from this acquisition. Synergies can be segmented into revenue synergies and cost synergies.

Let's start with revenue synergies first. One, it may be possible to cross-sell credit cards when selling banking services, or vice-versa. The reason for this is that a customer that is looking for banking services, is also probably looking for a credit card, since they are both related to personal finance. Two, acquiring a credit card company would give Bank Co. access to Nigeria Card's customer distribution channels. This would give Bank Co. access to new customer bases that they can sell to.

Next, let's move onto cost synergies. One, there could be a headcount reduction for redundant functions. For example, salesforce for the two companies could be reduced by training sales people how to sell both banking accounts and credit cards. Two, there could be a reduction of overhead, such as physical facilities and IT infrastructure.

Question 2: Bank Co. is hoping to break even from the acquisition costs within three years. Is this goal achievable? Here is some information:

The target price for the acquisition target is $14B.

Nigeria Card currently has 20M customers.

There are three different sources of revenue for credit cards.

- Annual fee: The annual fee for a credit card is $50 a year

- Credit card transaction revenue: When a consumer uses a credit card, Nigeria Card gets 3% of the total amount spent on the card. Let's assume that the average customer spends $15,000 a year.

- Credit card interest revenue: Interest gets charged on a credit card at a 20% per year interest rate. Let's assume that the average customer will get interest charged on $2,000 of spending per year.

There are four different types of costs for credit cards

- Credit card maintenance fee: It costs $10 a year to maintain credit card services. This includes cost of customer service, printing the credit card, replacing lost credit cards, and keeping the credit card information in the database.

- Customer bankruptcies: Let's assume that 5% of customers can't pay their credit card bills and that Nigeria Card loses $10,000 on each of these customers each year.

- Cost to borrow funds: Let's assume that it costs the credit card company 1% annual interest rate to borrow the money needed to fund the spend of customers. Let's assume that the average customer spends $15,000 a year, and the credit card company pays 1% annual interest rate on this.

- Fixed costs: Let's say that all of the fixed costs of the company total $800M a year.

In addition, let's project profits after the first year to increase 20% per year due to the growth of the company.

In other words, the information above can be used to calculate the profits during the first year. The second year's profits can be calculated by multiplying the first year's profits by 1.2. The third year's profits can be calculated by multiplying the second year's profits by 1.2, and so on.

(Sample answer is on the following page)

Answer to Question 2: The math is straight forward, but there are a lot of different parts to solving this problem. Let's take this one step at a time.

To calculate profit for the first year, we use the profit equation:

Profit = Revenue - Costs

Revenue:

- Annual fee: $50 * 20M customers = $1B

- Credit card transaction revenue: 3% * $15,000 * 20M customers = $9B

- Credit card interest revenue: 20% * $2,000 * 20M customers = $8B

Total revenue = $18B

Costs:

- Credit card maintenance fee: $10 * 20M customers = $200M

- Customer bankruptcies: 5% * 20M customers * $10,000 = $10B

- Cost to borrow funds: 1% * $15,000 * 20M customers = $3B

- Fixed costs: $800M

Total costs = $14B

Profit = $4B ($18B - $14B)

Therefore, the profit during the first year is $4B. We are given that profits grow by 20% each year due to an increase in customers.

Year one profit: $4B

Year two profit: $4.8B

Year three profit: $5.76B

After three years, the total profit will be **$14.56B**. The goal was to break even from the $14B in acquisition costs within three years. Therefore, the goal is achievable, with Bank Co. expected to bring in **$560M** in profit after the first three years.

Question 3: Instead of acquiring Nigeria Card, do you think Bank Co. would be able to offer attractive credit cards to customers on their own?

(Sample answer is on the following page)

Answer to Question 3: The answer could be either yes or no to this question. What matters is whether the candidate provides a reasonable, logical, and structured response. A sample response is shown below.

I don't think Bank Co. would be able to offer attractive credit cards on their own for the following three reasons.

One, credit cards are a different type of offering than checking or savings accounts. Credit cards have a tremendous amount of risk. Credit cards are products for consumer spending, while checking and savings accounts are products for consumer saving. For this reason, Bank Co. will have to be able to handle all of the risks that come with credit cards. When customers default on their credit card accounts, companies can end up losing a lot of money. I don't think Bank Co. has the knowledge or expertise to handle this.

Two, there are substantial technologies and capabilities needed in order to offer credit cards. There are complex database systems that need to get set up on the backend. In addition, Bank Co. does not have the other essential capabilities such as making the physical credit cards, designing attractive credit card incentives, and offering customer support for credit cards.

Third, Bank Co. will be missing a strong brand name in the credit card market. People know Bank Co. as a checking and savings account company, not as a credit card company.

For these three reasons, I think it would be very difficult for Bank Co. to offer credit cards on their own.

Conclusion: Let's say that the executive team of Bank Co. wants an interim update on whether or not they should acquire Nigeria Card. What do you say?

(Sample conclusion is on the following page)

Sample Conclusion: My working recommendation is that Bank Co. should acquire Nigeria Card for the following four reasons:

One, there will be significant synergies between Bank Co. and Nigeria Card if the acquisition were to happen. Revenue synergies include cross-selling products and having access to new customer bases. Cost synergies include consolidating headcount and reducing overhead costs.

Two, we did a breakeven analysis and determined it would take less than three years for Bank Co. to break even from the cost of acquisition. This is aligned with management's goals of breaking even within three years.

Three, the top three competitors are all offering credit cards. This suggests that Bank Co. should also offer credit cards if it does not want to be left behind. The top three banks all offering credit cards suggests that credit cards could be an essential part of the banking business.

Four, an acquisition should be made instead of developing a credit card offering organically in-house. This is because there are many technologies and capabilities that Bank Co. needs in order to offer attractive credit cards to customers. Examples include setting up a backend database and managing risk. By itself, Bank Co. does not have any of these.

For these four reasons, Bank Co. should acquire Nigeria Card.

For next steps, I would like to look into two things. One, I'd like to analyze the credit card market closer to determine if it is an attractive market. Two, I'd like to look more closely into Nigeria Card's financials and capabilities to understand if it is the most attractive acquisition target.

<u>Author Commentary</u>: This case is a bit more challenging than previous cases because it focuses and dives deeply into the credit card industry. You may not understand how credit cards work or be familiar with various terminology associated with the industry. This case tests how well you can jump into a specific industry and rationalize how the industry works.

For case interviews, interviewers do not expect candidates to have background knowledge in industries or topics that their case is on. Often times, interviewers will purposely choose an industry that people generally don't know or can't relate to (e.g., timeshares, data center equipment, waste disposal infrastructure). The important thing is to make sure to ask questions whenever you do not understand a term or a concept. The interviewer will not penalize you for this, and will provide further explanation to help you understand. Without understanding the terms and concepts involved, you are facing an uphill battle for solving the case.

Practice Case #4 – The Price is Right

Difficulty: Moderate

Pharma Co. is a large US pharmaceutical corporation. They research, develop, and manufacture drugs across a variety of therapeutic areas. They have recently finished developing a drug to treat arthritis.

Arthritis is a degenerative joint disease that affects the joints and surrounding tissues. Common symptoms of this disease include joint pain and stiffness, swelling, and decreased range of motion of affected joints.

The company expects that the drug will get FDA approval soon, and be ready for launch into the market. However, they are not sure what price to set for the drug. The CFO has hired you to help with this. What should the price of this new drug be?

(Sample framework is on the following page)

<u>Sample Framework</u>: One possible framework could look something like the following. The candidate does not need to have this exact framework, but should capture most of these points.

- Customer willingness to pay
    - How much is the customer willing to pay for this drug?
    - How much can the customer pay for the drug?
    - How does medical/drug insurance factor into how customers pay?

- Competitor pricing
    - Do competitors also offer a drug to treat Arthritis?
    - How effective/safe is their drug?
    - How much do competitors price their drug?

- Pharma Co.'s drug profitability
    - How much money has Pharma Co. invested in researching and developing the drug?
    - How much money does it cost to produce the drug?
    - In how much time is Pharma Co. looking to break even on the drug?

- Other pricing strategies
    - What other pricing strategies does Pharma Co. want to utilize?
        - Discounting for new customers
        - Bundling with other drugs
        - Subscription plan
    - How do these pricing strategies affect profit?

HACKING THE CASE INTERVIEW

Question 1: In order to determine how to best price the drug, let's examine the competitors' drugs for arthritis. The prices of their drugs are shown below, and are plotted against efficacy and safety risk.

Efficacy is how effective the drug is at reducing symptoms of arthritis. High efficacy means the drug works well at reducing symptoms and providing relief, while low efficacy means the drug does not do much for the consumer.

Safety risk is how safe the drug is for the customer to take in terms of minimal side effects and health implications. Low safety risk means the drug has almost no side effects and does not damage the consumer's overall health. High safety risk means the drug has serious side effects and may pose a threat for the consumer's health.

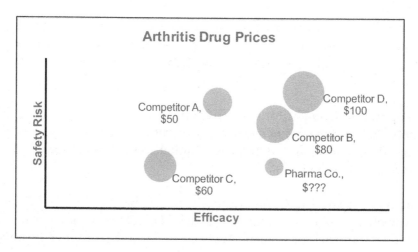

(Sample answer is on the following page)

Answer to Question 1: The candidate should come to the conclusion that Pharma Co.'s drug should be **priced higher than $80**. Depending on their reasoning, they could also say that the drug should be **priced higher than $100**.

To estimate the price of Pharma Co.'s drug, we need to look at the competitor drugs' efficacy, safety, and relative price. Generally, drugs that have high efficacy and low safety risk will be the drugs that are priced the highest. Let's compare each of the competitors' drugs to Pharma Co.'s drug.

Compared to Competitor A's drug, Pharma Co.'s drug has both higher efficacy and lower safety risk. Therefore, Pharma Co. has a much better drug and it should be priced higher than Competitor A's drug that is priced at $50.

Compared to Competitor B's drug, Pharma Co.'s drug has the same efficacy, but a lower safety risk. Therefore, Pharma Co. has the better drug and it should be priced higher than Competitor B's drug that is priced at $80.

Compared to Competitor C's drug, Pharma Co.'s drug has the same safety risk, and a higher efficacy. Therefore, Pharma Co. has the better drug and it should be priced higher than Competitor C's drug that is priced at $60.

Finally, compared to Competitor D's drug, Pharma Co.'s drug has a lower efficacy, but a lower safety risk. Therefore, it is hard to say whether the price of Pharma Co.'s drug should be higher or lower than $100. It would depend on whether a customer would prefer having a higher efficacy drug if that meant taking on a higher safety risk.

We can look at the ratio of safety risk to efficacy. Ideally, we would want a low ratio, which implies low safety risk and high efficacy. Comparing Pharma. Co to Competitor D, Pharma Co. has a much lower ratio of safety risk to efficacy. Therefore, one could make the case that Pharma Co.'s drug is better, and should be priced higher than Competitor D's drug that is priced at $100.

Question 2: Given the information about efficacy and safety risk in the previous question, how do you think Pharma Co. should market or brand their drug? What differentiates it from the four other drugs out there?

(Sample answer is on the following page)

Answer to Question 2: There are two possible answers to this question.

The candidate could say that Pharma Co.'s drug has the lowest safety risk in the market (tied with Competitor C). This could appeal to customers who are looking to avoid having serious side effects and health implications while relieving their arthritis symptoms.

The candidate could also say that Pharma Co.'s drug has the highest efficacy for the given amount of safety risk. In other words, Pharma Co.'s drug has the best "value" since it offers the lowest ratio of safety risk to efficacy. This could appeal to customers who are looking for the maximum amount of efficacy for the given amount of risk. This is analogous to the stock market, in which many investors want the highest returns for the given amount of risk.

Question 3: Next, let's look at what price Pharma Co. should price its drug at in order to break even from its investment within five years.

Pharma Co. has invested $4B in this drug, and each drug costs pennies to make. We can consider the costs of drug production to be a negligible amount. We don't know the number of customers in the US market, so you will need to determine that through market sizing. Assume that Pharma Co. will have a 20% market share of the arthritis drug market once they launch their drug. Assume that someone with arthritis will take the drug twice a year.

(Sample answer is on the following page)

Answer to Question 3: An example of a market sizing approach is given below.

Structure for estimating the arthritis drug market size:

- Start with the US population

- Segment the US population by age

- Estimate what percentage of each age group has arthritis

- Estimate what percentage of people with arthritis will take a drug vs. choose not to

Let's assume that the US population is 320M people. Let's divide the US population into four different segments: (0-20), (20-40), (40-60), and (60-80). Each segment has 80M people.

For (0-20), let's assume 0% of the population has arthritis. You typically develop arthritis as you get older, and this age segment is far too young to have such a disease.

For (20-40), let's also assume that 0% of the population has arthritis for the same reason as before. This age segment is still too young to have a significant prevalence of arthritis.

For (40-60), let's assume 10% of people have arthritis. This is based on personal experiences of hearing of aunts, uncles, and grandparents that have arthritis. Therefore, there are $8M people with arthritis in this segment. (10% * 80M)

For (60-80), let's assume that 20% of people have arthritis. As people get older, we'd expect more people to have the disease. Therefore, there are 16M people with arthritis in this segment. (20% * 80M)

Adding up the different age segments, we get 24M people with arthritis. (8M + 16M)

Next, let's assume that 75% of these people will take a drug to reduce the symptoms of arthritis. The other 25% will choose not to take a drug because of side effects or because they can tolerate their symptoms without any drug.

From this, we get 18M potential customers that take an arthritis drug.

Next, assuming we have a 20% market share, that brings the number of our own customers down to 3.6M.

Finally, we can set up a breakeven equation to estimate what the price of the drug should be to break even in 5 years.

The Breakeven Equation:

Quantity * (Price − Variable Costs) = Fixed Costs

We can calculate quantity first since we know the number of customers, how often they take the drug, and how long we have to break even

Quantity = 3.6M customers * 2 drugs a year * 5 years

Quantity = 36M units of drug

Variable Costs = $0 (each drug costs pennies to produce, which is negligible)

Fixed Costs = $4B

Plugging these values into the equation:

36M * Price = $4B

Price = ~$111

The drug needs to be **at least $111** in price in order for Pharma Co. to break even within 5 years.

Question 4: We'll move onto examining different customer segments' willingness to pay. Let's say that there are three segments of customers, each with a specific maximum that they are willing to pay for the drug. For a given customer segment, if the price of the drug is set above their maximum willingness to pay, that customer segment will not purchase the drug at all. Let's assume that we can only set one price point for the drug, which is the price all customers see and pay. We cannot price the drug differently for different customer segments. From the prior exercise, assume we have 3.6M customers and the breakeven price was ~$110.

Given the information below, what price point should the drug be set at?

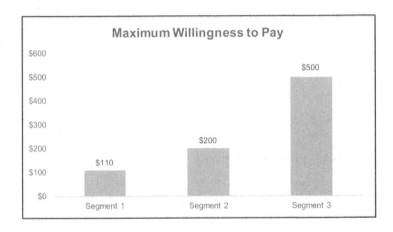

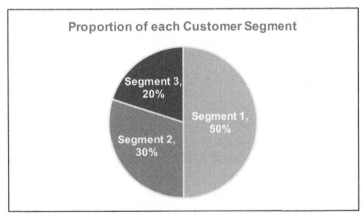

(Sample answer is on the following page)

Answer to Question 4: There are three different price points we can choose, $110, $200, or $500. If we set a price point above $500, no customers will buy the product. It would not make sense to price below $110, since all customers are willing to pay at least $110. Similarly, for prices between $110-$200, and $200-$500, it does not make sense to set a price in between those values since we can go up to the next highest maximum willingness to pay price point and get the same number of customers that will buy the drug.

If we set the price point at $110, all customers will purchase the drug, giving us $792M/year.

(3.6M customers * 100% customers * 2 drugs a year * 1 year * $110 = $792M/year)

If we set the price point at $200, customer segment 2 and customer segment 3 will purchase the drug, giving us $720M/year.

(3.6M customers * 50% customers * 2 drugs a year * 1 year * $200 = $720M/year)

If we set the price point at $500, only customer segment 3 will purchase the drug, giving us $720M/year.

(3.6M customers * 20% customers * 2 drugs a year * 1 year * $500 = $720M/year)

Therefore, it makes sense to price the drug at **$110** in order to get all customer segments to purchase the drug. This will create **$792M/year** in revenue for Pharma Co.

Conclusion: Let's say that the CFO wants a quick answer to how much they should price their arthritis drug for. What would you say?

(Sample conclusion is on the following page)

<u>Sample Conclusion</u>: I recommend that we price our arthritis drug at $110 for the following three reasons:

One, we did a breakeven analysis and determined that if we price the drug at $110, we will be able to break even in roughly 5 years. This meets our company goal.

Two, examining the different customer segments and their respective willingness to pay, we determined that $110 was the price point that would maximize revenue. If we price any higher, we lose customers, and revenues overall will decrease even though price has gone up.

Three, our drug price should be higher than that of our competitors because our drug has the highest efficacy for a given level of safety risk. The most expensive competitor drug is $100, and we should be able to price higher than that.

For these three reasons, $110 is the optimal price for the drug.

For next steps, I would like to look into two things. One, I'd like to look into ways to set a different price for different customer segments. This would allow us to further increase revenues. Two, I'd like to look into other pricing strategies such as discounting for new customers, bundling, or offering subscription pricing. These strategies may also further increase revenues.

Author Commentary: Especially for final-round interviews, expect to see various charts and figures with data. These can include: bar charts, bubble charts, line graphs, Venn diagrams, scatter plots, and flow charts. The interviewer will usually give you handouts with the charts and figures on them, but some interviewers are moving towards using interactive electronic tablets.

Make sure that you are familiar with all of the different ways that data can be presented and be able to interpret and analyze various charts and figures.

The "create your own bucket" was utilized for the last bucket in the framework. For final-round interviews, expect to be given more unusual business problems that require you to create one or two of your own buckets to address the case objectives.

Practice Case #5 – Diamonds are Forever

Difficulty: Moderate

Our client is Diamond Co., a jewelry manufacturer that specializes in making diamond jewelry. They are involved in all aspects of the diamond jewelry value chain, from mining the diamonds to manufacturing diamond rings, necklaces, and earrings.

Diamond Co. has recently experienced a decline in profitability over the past few years. The CEO has hired you to determine what is causing the decline in profitability. The CEO also wants recommendations on what Diamond Co. should do about it?

(Sample framework is on the following page)

<u>Sample Framework</u>: One possible framework could look something like the following. The candidate does not need to have this exact framework, but should capture most of these points.

- Financial situation
    - How has revenue changed during this time period?
        - Quantity
        - Price
    - How have costs changed during this time period?
        - Fixed Costs
        - Variable Costs

- Customer segments
    - Have customer preferences changed during this time period?
    - Do customers perceive or view our company differently than before?

- Competitive landscape of the diamond jewelry market
    - Have new competitors entered the market?
    - Are competitors doing something different than what they were doing previously?

- Diamond jewelry market
    - Has profitability declined for the diamond jewelry market overall?
    - Are there new government regulations affecting diamond mining or manufacturing?
    - Are there new technologies disrupting the diamond jewelry market?

Question 1: Let's look at diamond jewelry sales. Diamond Co. has three product lines of jewelry: rings, necklaces, and earrings. Looking at the information below, how much has the overall profit margin for Diamond Co. declined by? What is causing the decline in profit margin?

	Before		
Product	Percentage of Sales	Price sold at	Cost to produce
Rings	30%	$2,300	$1,150
Necklaces	30%	$1,800	$720
Earrings	40%	$1,000	$650

	Now		
Product	Percentage of Sales	Price sold at	Cost to produce
Rings	40%	$2,400	$1,200
Necklaces	20%	$1,700	$680
Earrings	40%	$1,200	$900

(Sample answer is on the following page)

Answer to Question 1: The overall profit margin for Diamond Co. is simply the weighted average of the profit margins for each product by the percentage of sales.

We will first calculate the profit margin of each product.

Profit margin = Profit / Price

For example, looking at rings from the "Before" table:

Profit margin = ($2,300 - $1,150) / $2300 = $1,150 / $2300 = 50%

This is repeated for all of the other calculations, and can be summarized in the table below.

Product	Before		Now	
	Percentage of Sales	Profit Margin	Percentage of Sales	Profit Margin
Rings	30%	50%	40%	50%
Necklaces	30%	60%	20%	60%
Earrings	40%	35%	40%	25%

Calculating the overall profit margin:

Before Profit Margin = (0.3 * 0.5) + (0.3 * 0.6) + (0.4 * 0.35)

Before Profit Margin = 47%

After Profit Margin = (0.4 * 0.5) + (0.2 * 0.6) + (0.4 * 0.25)

After Profit Margin = 42%

The overall profit margin for Diamond Co. has declined from **47%** to **42%**. The decline in profit margin is caused by two things. First, the profit margin for earrings has declined from 35% to 25%. Second, Diamond Co. is now selling more rings, which have a lower profit margin than necklaces, and selling fewer necklaces, which have a higher profit margin than rings.

Question 2: What percentage of the decline in overall profitability is caused by the shift of selling more rings and fewer necklaces? What percentage of the decline in overall profitability is caused by the decrease in profit margin for earrings?

(Sample answer is on the following page)

Answer to Question 2: We know that overall profit margins have declined from 47% to 42%, a difference of 5%.

To calculate what percentage of the decline in profitability is caused by the shift of selling more rings and fewer necklaces, we hold the profitability of earrings to be constant. This is shown in the table below, marked by a *.

	Before		Now	
Product	Percentage of Sales	Profit Margin	Percentage of Sales	Profit Margin
Rings	30%	50%	40%	50%
Necklaces	30%	60%	20%	60%
Earrings	40%	35%	40%	35%*

Before Profit Margin = 47%

After Profit Margin = (0.4 * 0.5) + (0.2 * 0.6) + (0.4 * 0.35)

After Profit Margin = 46%

Difference = 47% - 46% = **1%,** which is **20%** of the overall decline in profitability (1%/5%)

Similarly, for calculating what percentage of the decline in profitability is caused by the decrease in profit margin for earrings, we hold the percentage of sales of rings and necklaces constant. This is shown in the table below, marked by a *.

	Before		Now	
Product	Percentage of Sales	Profit Margin	Percentage of Sales	Profit Margin
Rings	30%	50%	30%*	50%
Necklaces	30%	60%	30%*	60%
Earrings	40%	35%	40%	25%

Before Profit Margin = 47%

After Profit Margin = (0.3 * 0.5) + (0.3 * 0.6) + (0.4 * 0.25)

After Profit Margin = 43%

Difference = 47% - 43% = **4%,** which is **80%** of the overall decline in profitability (4%/5%)

We previously calculated that profit margins declined from 47% to 42%, a difference of 5%. The shift of selling more rings and fewer necklaces accounted for **20%** of this overall decline. The decrease in profit margin for earrings accounted for **80%** of this overall decline.

Question 3: Let's look at why we are selling fewer necklaces. The table below shows information about the necklace prices for Diamond Co. vs. the other competitors.

What insights can you draw from this table as to why Diamond Co. is selling fewer necklaces? What should Diamond Co. do to solve this?

Company	Necklace Price	Quantity Sold
Diamond Co.	$1,700	500
Competitor A	$11,000	4,000
Competitor B	$600	10,000
Competitor C	$20,000	2,000
Competitor D	$300	30,000
Competitor E	$17,000	3,000
Competitor F	$500	25,000

(Sample answer is on the following page)

Answer to Question 3: Looking at the table, there are two distinct price groups.

Competitor A, C, and E seem to sell high-end necklaces at a price point of $11,000, $20,000, and $17,000. Competitors B, D, and F seem to sell low-end necklaces at a price point of $600, $300, and $500. Diamond Co. lies in the middle of this price spectrum, at $1,700.

Diamond Co. is getting squeezed out of the diamond necklace market. There are two distinct price ranges that customers seem to purchase from. The "high-end" range from $11,000 - $20,000 or the "low-end" range from $300 - $600. Customers do not seem to want to purchase a "mid-range" diamond necklace that lies in between these two.

To solve this, Diamond Co. should change the price of its diamond necklaces to fall into one of these two ranges. We know that their necklace costs $680 to produce. Because of this, Diamond Co. should not sell in the "low-end" of the market because that price range is $300 - $600, and Diamond Co. will not be profitable. Therefore, Diamond Co. should price its diamond necklace higher, closer to the $11,000 - $ 20,000 range. This may increase quantity of necklaces sold, while also significantly improving profit margins.

Question 4: Looking at the information we have on earrings, what can you conclude about why its profit margin has decreased? What are some ways to improve its profit margin?

(Sample answer is on the following page)

<u>Answer to Question 4:</u> Profit margins for earrings have declined because costs have increased at a faster rate than price has increased. We can improve profit margins by increasing price or decreasing costs.

- Increase Price
    - Invest more in marketing the earrings as an ultra-premium product to justify a higher price
    - Offer limited edition earrings in order to artificially decrease supply, which may increase the market price
    - Redesign the earring into a new style to sell at a higher price

- Decrease Costs
    - Decrease variable costs
        - Renegotiate purchasing price for raw materials used to make earrings (e.g. the silver, gold, or other metal that is part of the earring)
        - Use a smaller quantity of diamonds to manufacture the earrings
        - Use lower quality diamonds in the earrings
    - Decrease fixed costs
        - Invest in new equipment or technology that is more cost efficient to mine diamonds and produce earrings
        - Renegotiate distributor or retailer contracts
        - Renegotiate salaries

A common mistake that occurs among candidates is confusing profit with profitability.

<u>Conclusion</u>: The CEO wants a quick answer to why profitability has declined and what the company should do about it. What do you say?

(Sample conclusion is on the following page)

<u>Sample Conclusion</u>: Diamond Co. is experiencing a decline in profitability for two reasons: 1) profit margins for earrings have declined from 35% to 25%, and 2) Diamond Co. is selling more rings, which have a lower profit margin than necklaces, and fewer necklaces. The first reason is responsible for 80% of the decline in profitability.

To address this, I recommend the following two actions.

One, Diamond Co. should increase the price that it sells its necklaces for. We are being squeezed out of this market because most competitors sell their necklaces at either a "low-end" or "high-end" price range. Our company prices necklaces in between these two ranges, and customers seem to want either a cheap necklace or a very expensive necklace. They do not want necklaces that fall in between.

Two, Diamond Co. can work on improving profitability on their earrings. They can do this by either increasing price or decreasing costs. Diamond Co. can increase price through offering limited edition earrings, redesigning the earring look or style, or investing in marketing the earrings as an ultra-premium product. They can decrease costs by reducing fixed costs and/or variable costs. Fixed costs can be reduced by investing in more efficient technology to mine diamonds and produce earrings or by renegotiating salaries or contracts. Variable costs can be reduced by using a smaller quantity or lower quality of diamonds for their earrings.

For next steps, I would like to look into the following two things. One, I'd look into what price necklaces should be set at to maximize profits. Two, I'd look into how to improve profitability of rings, which we have not looked into yet.

Author Commentary: For this case, the math calculation for Question 2 is on the more difficult side. Whenever you get a complex math problem, it is important to try to break it down into smaller pieces of calculations so that you don't get lost in the numbers. Question 2 basically asks for two different drivers, what percentage of decline in profits is caused by each?

We can break down this calculation in the following way:

- Determine the overall decline in profitability if both drivers occur (this was answered in Question 1)

- Determine the decline in profitability if only Driver 1 occurs

- Divide the decline in profitability if only Driver 1 occurs by the overall decline in profitability (this is the percentage of profitability decline caused by Driver 1)

- Subtract the previous answer from 100% to determine the decline in profitability caused by Driver 2 (Driver 1 + Driver 2 must be responsible for 100% of the decline in profitability)

- Alternatively, we can repeat the first three bullets for Driver 2

Another common mistake candidates make is confusing profit with profitability/profit margin. If you're not sure which of these metrics have declined, make sure to ask the interviewer. These two metrics can lead the case in completely different directions.

Remember that:

Profit = Revenue ($) − Costs ($)

Profit Margin = Profit ($) / Revenue ($)

Final Thoughts

You now know exactly what to expect during the case interview. You know what interviewers are looking for, and what to do and say for each part of the case interview. You know the single framework that you need to memorize in order to efficiently develop unique and effective frameworks for every case. You have practiced and sharpened up your basic math skills while learning or reviewing basic business knowledge.

There is more learning to be done. I recommend getting with your case interview partner and practicing as many cases as you have the time for. Every case that you do makes you a stronger, more competitive candidate and gets you closer to your dream job offer. Interviewing for consulting firms is a very competitive process, and you want to do as many case interviews as you can to put yourself in the best position to succeed.

While preparing for case interviews can take a significant amount of time, if consulting is truly the job that you want, the time invested is worth it. What separates a candidate that gets multiple consulting job offers from one who doesn't get any is the amount of time invested. You need to invest the time and have the discipline to follow through.

Case interviews can be quite fun. You get to solve interesting and complex business problems in under an hour. If you feel yourself enjoying doing practice cases, then that is a good sign that you will have a great time with consulting as your profession.

I wish you the best of luck.

If you found this book helpful and want even more detailed explanations, examples, practice problems, real practice cases, and strategies, I've created a one-week case interview online crash course that can be found at **HackingTheCaseInterview.com**

The goal of the crash course is to help you pass your upcoming interview in the shortest amount of time possible. It is an all-inclusive course that contains (1) all of the strategies and knowledge you need to know, and (2) all of the practice problems and practice cases you need to do to be competent.

Overview of the One-Week Case Interview Crash Course

- Engage with 50+ concise video lessons that consolidate hundreds of hours of knowledge and experience

- Hone your case interview skills through 20 real, full-length practice cases, with detailed solutions and feedback

- Learn an advanced framework strategy to tackle non-traditional case problems typically given in final round interviews

- Review and practice understanding and interpreting the 10 types of charts and graphs you'll see in a case interview

- Practice and refine your newly learned strategies with quality practice problems in every section

If you found this book helpful, I highly recommend checking out **HackingTheCaseInterview.com** to take what you've learned in this book to the next level.

About the Author

Taylor Warfield is a former Bain consultant, case interviewer, and case workshop leader. His top-selling case interview prep book, "Hacking the Case Interview," has helped 3,000+ students in 13+ countries. His book, online course, and coaching have helped hundreds of candidates land job offers at top consulting firms such as McKinsey, Bain, and BCG. He is the founder of **HackingTheCaseInterview.com**

Made in United States
North Haven, CT
24 August 2022